THE GLAMOUR OF BELLVILLE SASSOON

DAVID SASSOON
SINTY STEMP
FOREWORD BY SUZY MENKES

© 2009 SINTY STEMP

World copyright reserved

ISBN 978-1-85149-575-7

The right of Sinty Stemp to be identified as
author of this work has been asserted by her
in accordance with the Copyright, Designs
and Patents Act 1988

Every effort has been made to secure permission
to reproduce the images contained within this
book, and we are grateful to the individuals
and institutions who have assisted in this task.
Any errors are entirely unintentional, and the
details should be addressed to the publisher.

British Library Cataloguing-in-Publication Data

A catalogue record for this book is available
from the British Library

Book and cover designed and typeset by
John and Orna Designs, London

Printed in China

Published in England by ACC Editions,
an imprint of the Antique Collectors' Club Ltd.,
Woodbridge, Suffolk

ACC EDITIONS

CONTENTS

FOREWORD BY SUZY MENKES 4

PREFACE BY DAVID SASSOON 7

BEGINNINGS 8

ROYAL COLLEGE OF ART 20

BELTING ALONG WITH BELLVILLE 32

SIGN OF THE TIMES —
BELLVILLE SASSOON THOUGH THE DECADES 62

ROYALS 154

QUEEN FOR A DAY —
BELLVILLE BRIDES 226

JEWELS AND BALLS 250

VOGUE PATTERNS 276

NEW HORIZONS 290

ACKNOWLEDGMENTS 300

INDEX 302

FOREWORD BY SUZY MENKES Five Princesses – Anne, Alexandra, Diana, Margaret and Michael – make a royal roster as long and as glamorous as the bridal trains David Sassoon has created for 50 years.

But the half century since the young graduate from London's Royal College of Art joined Belgravia dressmaker Belinda Bellville has more significance than just another fashion anniversary. For Sassoon's illustrious career holds up a mirror to changing British society.

The year 1958 was the last when debutantes were presented at court – but it was not quite the end of aristocratic elegance. The 17-year-old Camilla Shand – the future Duchess of Cornwall – who 'came out' in 1965, was dressed by Bellville Sassoon. And while today's models might marry rock stars, a different class of beau had kissed the fine-boned cheeks of Bronwyn Pugh (who married Lord Astor) and Fiona Campbell-Walter, who became Baroness von Thyssen.

Yet, in some ways, Bellville Sassoon, set up in a former stable rather than in a gilded mansion dripping with chandeliers, anticipated the modernizing of society in the 1960s. That was when the class system splintered and the jet set took off. Evangeline Bruce, the great American political hostess, even brought to the Bellville fashion house Jacqueline Kennedy with her sister Lee Radziwill. In the first stirrings of celebrity, the house dressed upcoming film stars Julie Christie and Catherine Deneuve.

The social butterflies fluttered on throughout the 'swinging sixties'. Sassoon remembers creating Lady Annabel Birley's gown for one of the 20th century's last great society events: the Proust Ball held by Marie-Hélène de Rothschild in 1971. Although Bellville does have a more democratic side as the only British designer for Vogue Patterns for over 40 years.

When Lady Diana Spencer exploded on to the royal scene at the start of the 1980s she brought a new sparkle to society.

'She did love romantic things,' says Sassoon of the future Princess of Wales, whose engagement photographs featured his demure sailor-collared dress. He dressed her in a salmon pink going away outfit and created the vivid flower print for what the Princess called her 'caring' dress, worn to cheer up children in hospital.

4

The discreet dressmaker was no stranger to royal circles – even if his first visit to Buckingham Palace, to fit a dress on the fledgling Princess Anne, saw him trip over the corgis' water bowls while bowing to the Queen. (Her Majesty ignored the gaff, but had previously asked if her daughter's dress could go in the wash!)

Sassoon recalls the Duchess of Kent handing him a piece of lace that had been treasured by Queen Victoria. He made the wedding dress for Princess Michael of Kent in 1978, as well as gowns for society daughters. No wonder that America dubbed the company 'The Wedding Bell-villes' and that New York's Bergdorf Goodman filled all its store windows with the British brand's bridal gowns.

When Belinda Bellville retired in 1982, there were still seamstresses to make exquisite one-off creations. They included hand-painted coats which were auctioned at Christies and ultimately given to the Victoria and Albert Museum.

Couture may now be hanging by a silken thread, but Lorcan Mullany, the Irish-born designer who joined the company in 1987, has played an important role in developing the ready-to-wear collections. His designs are sold successfully across the world under the Bellville Sassoon Lorcan Mullany label.

The company is not mired in its grand past but finds fresh clients, like the American cultural philanthropist Blaine Trump and Mrs Galen Weston. There are also young actresses, singers and television presenters, including Kelly Brook, Leona Lewis and Rosamund Pike.

The royal connection continues. When President Sarkozy of France came on a state visit to the United Kingdom, Sassoon could look with pride at the Princess Royal wearing the Wedgwood patterned jacket he had designed. In its blue and white beading it was a spirited nod to English culture and history – and a streamlined style for an active, modern, hard-working Princess.

Bellville Sassoon is that rare British house which is happy – even in this era of 'fast' fashion and cool clothes – to create outfits as a gift to women to make them look their best.

For Belinda
Without whom all this
Would never have happened

PREFACE BY DAVID SASSOON I have been privileged to enjoy a career that spans over fifty years, doing what I most enjoy, designing glamorous clothes for some of the most beautiful and charismatic women in the world. I have worked from Couture to ready-to-wear with a wonderful team of talented professionals who have become my 'family' and friends; without them the company would not be what it is today.

Belinda Bellville who founded the company was my business partner for twenty-five years; she was my inspiration and mentor - without her there would be no Bellville Sassoon. After Belinda retired in 1982, Lorcan Mullany joined the company and for the last twenty-one years we have worked very closely. Lorcan brings to the collection his own personal stamp, which has extended our range and brought new fans from all over the world. We sell our collections in America, Asia, the Middle East, France, Italy, Spain, Germany and the UK. Lorcan is the way forward for the company and we have many exciting new projects planned together.

I have enjoyed working with Sinty Stemp who has worked tirelessly on this book, which has been a rediscovery of my early career and my journey through the turbulent world of creative fashion. I have enjoyed the journey and this book is about how it all began and developed. My thanks to Orna Frommer-Dawson for designing a stylish and colourful book. My special thanks go also to Felicity Green who has nurtured and encouraged this project from the start.

I dedicate this book to all the lovely ladies who wear our glamorous dresses.

7

BEGINNINGS

BEGINNINGS I can't remember a time when I was not interested in fashion. At a very early age I was dressing up my younger sister Marguerite, using anything I could lay my hands on, old sheets and even bits of blackout material. It was 1943, she was seven and I was eleven, and we were living in Llandudno in north Wales – my parents had moved us all out of our London home when the bombs began to drop.

Even as a schoolboy, living among the privations of war, I felt a longing for real glamour and colour. I am sure this came from my exotic oriental background: my father, Gourgi Sassoon, came from Basra and my mother, Victoria, came from Baghdad. They married and came to England in about 1925. Ours was a large and happy family – I was born in Highbury, north London in 1932, the fourth of six children, three boys and three girls, all of us born in England. First came my sister Mollie, then Victor, then Laurette, then me, then Ronald, and lastly Marguerite. Being among the youngest, I was particularly close to Marguerite, who was the baby of the family. We were inseparable as children, both naughty, and always getting into mischief. Though it was not intentional, destruction and havoc seemed to follow in my wake. My mother despaired of me, and I kept hearing the words, "Whatever will become of you?" My memory of the family home in London was that it was completely Middle Eastern, filled with colour and decoration. Even the meals we ate at home were Middle Eastern, as my father would not eat European food. All my young life I was surrounded by wonderful Persian carpets – but I yearned for Wilton and Axminster!

Then I discovered Hollywood glamour, and it could not have come at a better time for me. The war had led to endless restrictions, and rationing had become a way of life – there were queues for everything and we all had to 'make do and mend'. Films were my consolation and when I could I used to escape to the local cinema, first in Llandudno, and afterwards back in London. My special heartthrob was the actress, Merle Oberon, the number one film star of the day. I thought she was wonderful, the most beautiful, the most exquisite of all the stars – to me she eclipsed all others. I loved the way she looked and dressed, she had such poise and presence; she really was quite different from the rest. As an ardent young fan I avidly collected photographs and press cuttings about her, and as a young teenager I used to keep a picture of her in my wallet. I first fell in love with Merle Oberon when she played Cathy to Laurence Olivier's Heathcliff in the 1939 film of *Wuthering Heights*. A little later, in *A Song To Remember* (1945), a film about Chopin's life, she played George Sand and wore marvellous period dresses. My love affair continued in 1954 when I saw her as Napoleon's Joséphine in *Désirée*. These films were my first introduction to romance, but I think I loved the costumes almost as much as I loved Merle! Imperceptibly they were adding to my fashion 'vocabulary'; they fed my love of glamour and first sparked my interest in historical costume.

These films were just one part of my early fascination with clothes. My mother was also keen on fashion, and I liked to hear stories about her life in Baghdad. Her family was related to Flora Sassoon, who was an important figure in the social world of Edwardian Sephardic Jewish society and part of the Sassoon banking dynasty. My mother's sister, Violet also married a Sassoon. As children and then as young women, my mother and her two sisters always wore fashionable clothes. When flesh stockings were introduced in the early 1920s my mother had some. She wore them in the street one day, and when she went into the Arab quarter in Baghdad she had to cover herself with a burka. As she passed a group of Arab boys, one of them lay on the ground and pinched her ankle as she walked by, calling out to the other boys, "They ARE stockings!" – they were quite a novelty in those days.

OVERLEAF LEFT My sister Marguerite in a silver organza cocktail dress, one of my early designs, 1955 OVERLEAF RIGHT My favourite portrait, Lady Aline Sassoon, 1907 by John Singer Sargent [Private Collection/The Bridgeman Art Library]

Z. G. Donatossian-Baghdad

My father Gourgi Sassoon Baghdad 1923

My Mother Victoria standing on the right, with her two sisters Violet and Rosa Baghdad 1923.

One of my earliest visual memories, and something that has stayed with me all my life, is a striking portrait of Lady Aline Sassoon, painted in 1907 by the society artist, John Singer Sargent. It is a marvellous evocation of the *belle époque*, which became my favourite historical era thanks to the power of this painting, and I am always struck by how Sargent has managed to capture his sitter's dramatic costume. The portrait has such vitality, such dash and verve and romance, it has remained an abiding inspiration to me in my work. It's the image that somehow I always come back to.

My mother decided that she did not want to remain in Baghdad, and married my father only on condition that they came to live in England. They came over by steamer and my mother travelled in style with a full set of Louis Vuitton trunks containing her beautiful trousseau. The trunks were stored in the hold for the long journey, and the damp warped all her handmade shoes. Twenty years later, a lot of the trousseau ended up in ten-year-old Marguerite's dressing-up box, and we had a wonderful time dressing up in them. There was a wonderful selection of velvet dresses, pintucked silk bodices and camisoles, and I used to enjoy 'customising' these, sewing on ribbon bows, to make costumes out of them for Marguerite.

Back in London in 1945, the war was finally over and the blackout material all came down from the windows, which meant I had an abundance of 'fabric' with which to practise. I used to love looking at my mother's copies of *Vogue*, which were another early source of inspiration. They opened my eyes to that longed-for world of glamour and luxury. I would pore over them for hours to get ideas for my own 'creations' – designs which I drew for my mother and sisters. We would all go along to the dressmakers and I would help them choose fabrics and then watch intently while they were pinned and fitted into my 'designs'. It was always a treat, and brought to life all those glamorous images I had seen in the pages of my mother's magazines.

Films and fashion might have been my passions, but I still had my education to deal with, and school was not a happy place for me. I soon realised I was never going to excel academically, and this was a great worry to my parents. Every one of my brothers and sisters was successful at school, and I was the only one in the family who was a disappointment. Nobody knew about such things then, but in fact it was later discovered that I was very dyslexic. However, I was always ambitious and determined to star, and this lack of achievement at school only spurred me on. I had always wanted to be good at *something*, and now I developed a killer instinct to succeed; but it would be in another field more suited to my talents.

Originally, my love of films meant that I wanted to be an actor, but my parents were totally against the idea. Although I wasn't academic, I had a sympathetic drama teacher who encouraged me to be in all the school plays. One of my command performances was as David in *David Copperfield*, "If you please, aunt I am your nephew... I am David Copperfield, of Blunderstone, in Suffolk – where you came the night when I was born and saw my dear mama. I have been very unhappy since she died." At this point I had to produce some heart-rending tears and always managed to produce a tragic sob. Another of my dramatic triumphs was my Oberon in *A Midsummer Night's Dream*, and I told everyone at school I was going to be a famous actor. It was this sympathetic drama teacher who helped me apply to RADA (the Royal Academy of Dramatic Art). It was a surprise to everyone, apart from me, when I was successful and won a place.

However, my father, a very Middle Eastern gentleman, was not going to have one of his sons treading the boards. He put his paternal foot down firmly. My parents were then presented with my second choice of career: fashion. They considered this the lesser of two evils. When

OPPOSITE PAGE A fervent film fan in my youth, the elegant Merle Oberon, right, was always my favourite actress and I love this quirky photograph of her. Forty years later, Merle Oberon entered my life again. I had always wanted to design a dress for her and I regretted that I had not been able to fulfil this wish. So I was thrilled to hear from Lucienne Phillips, who had a well-known designer label boutique in Knightsbridge, that Merle Oberon had bought one of my dresses from her in the '80s. I had 'dressed' Merle Oberon after all!

I decided to enrol on a fashion course at Hammersmith School of Art my father still wasn't best pleased, but ironically my lack of academic skills now worked in my favour. My parents, despairing that I had no other abilities, felt that they had no alternative but to go along with my choice.

I was seventeen when I first started at Hammersmith School of Art and I was the only boy there; fashion at that time was not a career that men really went into, hence my father's misgivings. There was no dress-making class within the art college, so we had to go next door to a trade school where they trained dressmakers for the fashion industry. Here, I was taught dressmaking one day a week, and to begin with I was pretty hopeless!

I tried hard and practised what I learnt on my younger sister, so Marguerite became my muse and mannequin. My first proper attempts at dressmaking were made for her and she would stand patiently in front of a mirror while I tried to pin together my latest efforts. Marguerite blossomed into a real beauty with a figure to match, so it was a pleasure to make things for her. She was always beautifully dressed – thanks to me – and when I think back to that time, during my college years Marguerite had an amazing wardrobe for a girl of her age.

My mother understood my love of fashion and encouraged my ambition. She was a bit like the matchmaking Mrs Bennett in Jane Austen's novel, *Pride and Prejudice*, very keen on getting her daughters settled with suitable husbands. Every weekend she would get me on the sewing machine, running up little numbers to tempt the host of eligible bachelors who were always queuing up to date my lovely sisters, Mollie and Marguerite. But then at the end of my first year at Hammersmith my fashion life came to an abrupt halt when I had to do my National Service. I joined the Air Force and after my initial training I was posted to Egypt at the time of the Suez Crisis and spent eighteen months in a tent in the desert. Even as Airman Sassoon I was determined not to lose touch with fashion, so I had *Vogue* and *Harper's Bazaar* sent out to me, and when it was time for me to return, I had them all packed up and shipped back to London. By the time I was eventually demobbed I had been away for two years. Although I was delighted to get back to college, all the students I had initially started out with were no longer there, as they had already graduated. So I had to start all over again with a new team.

I spent a further two years at Hammersmith. Then, in my last year there, quite by chance, I saw a feature in the popular magazine, *Picture Post*, all about the newly established School of Fashion Design at the Royal College of Art, which kindled my ambition. That was it; from then on I had a burning desire to go there and, with the help and encouragement of my teacher, Joanne Brogden, I prepared my portfolio and sat an entrance exam for the Royal College.

I was the only one from my class to apply. It was every student's dream to get on to this course. Places were strictly limited, and very few students

16

My Sister Marguerite and I Wales 1942

My Sister Mollie 1953

In the Air Force Posted to Egypt 1951

were accepted – only seven in my year. The competition to gain a coveted place was intense, but I had done it. Encouraged by Joanne Brogden, I had the temerity to invite Madge Garland – the formidable Principal of the Fashion School at the Royal College of Art – to my final show at Hammersmith; and to my surprise she came. When I met her afterwards she was kind enough to say she was impressed by my work, and I am sure this worked in my favour. I also had to go before an interview panel at the Royal College, which I knew would be biased towards traditional fine art. When they asked me who my favourite painter was, I said proudly, "John Singer Sargent" and told them all about the Lady Aline Sassoon portrait.

By this time I had managed to persuade my father that fashion was a profession with good prospects. Sadly, he died suddenly during my last term at Hammersmith. I had already taken the entrance exam to the Royal College of Art, but it was very poignant for me that my father never knew I had been accepted. He died in the spring of 1955 and five months later I was starting my first term. I knew I was going to the best college in the country with his blessing, and my mother's support meant a lot to me. When I started at the Royal College of Art she bought me my first sewing machine and a dress stand. Fashion was going to be the passion of my life.

18

ABOVE A long taffeta evening coat I designed for my graduation show at the Hammersmith School of Art, 1955 LEFT The same taffeta evening coat makes its debut on the catwalk RIGHT Working with fellow student, Pearl Caplan, at Hammersmith School of Art

ROYAL COLLEGE OF ART

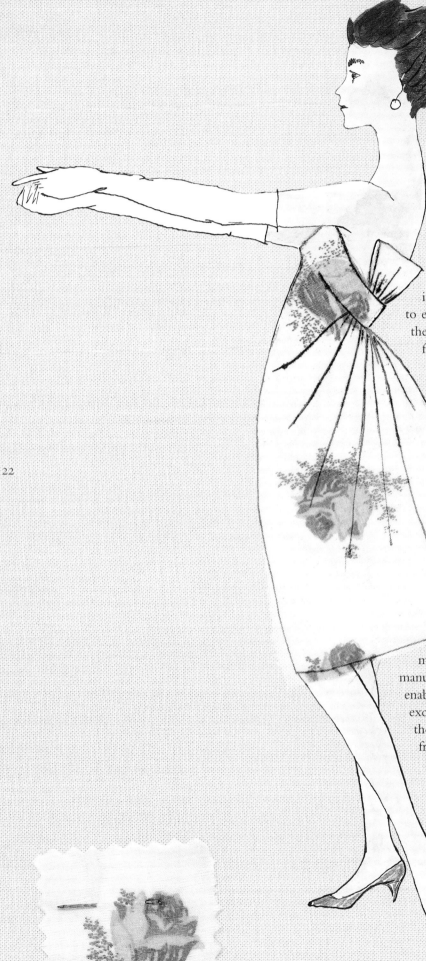

THE ROYAL COLLEGE OF ART When I started at the Royal College of Art there was a new focus on the importance of design. The Festival of Britain in 1951 had celebrated the role of contemporary design and brought it centre stage in the nation's consciousness. As a result, the Royal College was a beacon of hope and excitement in the emerging confidence of fifties Britain. The Fashion School was integral to the drive for export success in the post-war era, when the need to earn foreign currency and develop trade links was vital to re-energising the country's economy. My three years there, from 1955 to 1958, were very fulfilling and happy. My mind was opening to the magic of fashion. It all felt absolutely right; I had found my place in the world.

The first thing I noticed was how different it was from my old college. Hammersmith was a provincial school by comparison; the Royal College was a professional college. The real difference was that when you got to the Royal College there were no full-time teachers. Instead, we were taught by professionals from the industry itself. So the pattern cutter from Horrocks would come in, the tailor from Digby Morton would come in, the shoe designer from Saxones would come in. It was the best possible preparation for a career in fashion.

I would not have missed this experience for the world. The next three years at the Royal College represented a very important part of my life. I was given a professional grounding and an entrée to the leading fashion companies: designers, manufacturers, and experts in every field of the industry. We had an opportunity to meet, work with, and learn from the most important ready-to-wear manufacturers as well as the great couturiers. All doors were opened to us – enabling us to gain a wealth of experience that was so precious and so exclusive it was like gold dust. I look back with appreciation, not only for the level of skill I acquired, but also for the great encouragement I received from all my tutors.

The School of Fashion occupied an elegant five-storey period townhouse at 20 Ennismore Gardens, South Kensington. Our work-rooms were on the first floor with wonderful light from three large French windows and it was a marvellous place in which to work. We had a fantastic couture-trained teacher from Vienna, Anna Frankel. She was an amazing toileist, and I really came into my own when she taught us how to drape fabric on the stand, which just seemed to come naturally to me. The Principal would set us design projects, which were quite varied: a wardrobe for the Queen's state visit to Paris, ballgowns, even theatre costumes. Anything to do with eveningwear and glamour was my favourite. For one project we had to design a wardrobe for Marilyn Monroe. Our efforts were judged by the Incorporated

MADGE GARLAND

JANEY IRONSIDE

JOANNE BROGDEN

Society couturier, John Cavanagh, and to my absolute delight, he thought my designs were the best. But it wasn't just couturiers who came to judge our work, our final-year assessor was the Head of Design at Marks & Spencer.

I am privileged to have been taught by all three heads of the Fashion School during my time there. They were three of the most important figures in the world of fashion education, and all three were highly respected within the industry itself. My first professor was Madge Garland, the awe-inspiring founder of the Fashion School, which had been inaugurated in 1948. Known as Lady Ashton in her married life, she was very grand, with a great sense of chic and style. A former editor of *Vogue*, she dressed exclusively in couture; she looked and acted every inch the part – a real fashion professional. She favoured designs by Molyneux and always wore hats by Aage Thaarup (the royal milliner), Simone Mirman, or Rudolf – the three big names in millinery in the '50s. I liked and admired Madge Garland and thought she was rather amazing.

The 1950s was a decade still defined by the strict rules and protocol of 'The Establishment' and, although we were students, attitudes were still very formal at the Royal College of Art. All the male students had to wear a suit when we attended a fashion show, and all the girls had to wear a pair of white gloves, which they kept ready in their workroom drawer. In my first year I was in the Royal College's annual theatre production: Chekhov's *Uncle Vanya*. For my role of Ilya Ilyich Telegin I powdered my hair white to look like an old man. I thought it looked great and couldn't be bothered to wash it out every day. Madge Garland did not approve and I was sent for and told to go home and wash my hair, "Now, my child," she exclaimed in a brisk tone, "You're not in the circus now!" I was upset until I heard that Cecil Beaton had been in the audience and had told the producer I looked very distinguished!

At the end of each Christmas term the Fashion School hosted a formal cocktail party and the pale pink taffeta dress I made for my sister Marguerite was much admired. The early '50s was the era of the big net petticoat worn under full-skirted dresses, inspired by Christian Dior's 'New Look'. I remember making Marguerite one of these huge net petticoats. It must have had at least fifteen layers and when it flopped a bit I just added another layer or two. When we went on our Continental holidays together it needed its own special bag as it was far too big to fit into her suitcase. But it was worth it, it was an absolute must to boost up her dresses when we went to ritzy nightclubs in Italy and France, and she was wearing it when we saw the Duke and Duchess of Windsor on Capri.

I was very impressed by the fact that Madge Garland knew people like Cecil Beaton and the Sitwells, and had been painted in the '20s by the famous society painter, Marie Laurencin. Although she never directly taught us, she was very dynamic nonetheless and a great asset to the college and to all the students. She was on the advisory boards of companies like Courtaulds and acted as a consultant to the very successful West Cumberland Silk Mills, and the famous textile designer, Miki Sekers. She was also involved with the Incorporated Society of London Fashion

23

OPPOSITE PAGE Sketch of rose print organza dress from my Royal College final year show, 1958 ABOVE, FROM LEFT My three Royal College mentors: Madge Garland by Cecil Beaton; Janey Ironside [by kind permission Virginia Ironside]; Joanne Brogden by Fred Duberry

Royal College of Art project work: three designs, each fully accessorised, for the Queen's state visit to Paris, 1957 LEFT Formal evening dress with attached train MIDDLE Elegant day dress with hat to match RIGHT The royal finale: crinoline-style ballgown worn with long white evening gloves and a diamond tiara

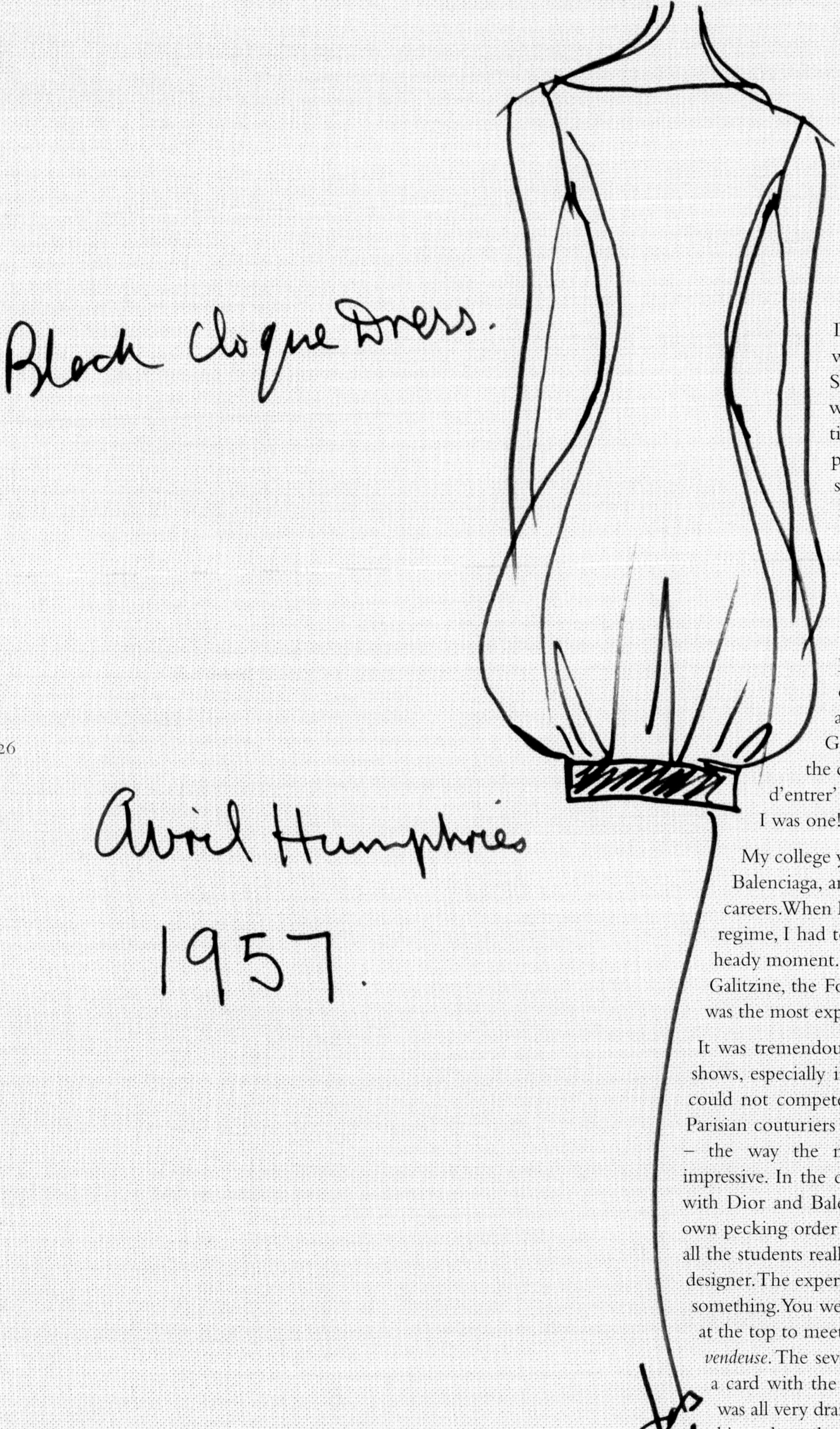

Black Cloque Dress.

Avril Humphries

1957.

Designers, the group of British couturiers which modelled itself on the Chambre Syndicale in Paris. Through these contacts we would get donations of fabrics and introductions for student placements. She was ideally placed to foster closer links with the professional fashion world, persuading leading industry insiders to serve as tutors. Through her, we went to shows by many of the Incorporated Society members, among them John Cavanagh, Digby Morton, Ronald Paterson, Mattli, Michael, and Hardy Amies, and were able to see at first hand the cream of English couture. Best of all, however, was the opportunity to see the couture shows in Paris and Italy – again entirely thanks to Madge Garland. She received personal invitations from the designers and would give these precious 'cartes d'entrer' to her favourite students – and, fortunately, I was one!

My college years were Paris's vintage couture years – Dior, Balenciaga, and Jean Dessès were all at the height of their careers. When I went to the shows as part of Madge Garland's regime, I had to write reports afterwards and drink in every heady moment. In Italy I saw the collections of Princess Irene Galitzine, the Fontana Sisters, and of Roberto Capucci, who was the most experimental of the Italian couturiers.

It was tremendously inspiring and exhilarating to go to these shows, especially in Paris; the Incorporated Society in London could not compete with what Paris had to offer. The way the Parisian couturiers presented their shows was almost like a ballet – the way the models looked and moved was incredibly impressive. In the couture world there was a definite hierarchy, with Dior and Balenciaga at the apex. As students we had our own pecking order for the couturiers. When we were at college all the students really admired Balenciaga – he was the designer's designer. The experience of going to a Balenciaga show was quite something. You went up to the salon in a padded leather lift and at the top to meet you would be the terrifying *directrice* or head *vendeuse*. The severe model girls, who never smiled, each held a card with the number of the style they were showing – it was all very dramatic, very graphic. Balenciaga was known for his sculptural cuts, his famous sleeves (all worn with gloves), his famous necks with rosette buttons, his famous hats – his were the most expensive clothes in Paris and, for me, the most beautifully made.

THIS PAGE Sketch of the balloon-skirted dress designed for my final year show in 1958. OPPOSITE The dress in black cloqué, worn by model Avril Humphries, pictured on the steps of the Royal College of Art, post-show

The grandest couture house of all was Jean Dessès, which had a large sweeping staircase and was all old-school plush; going there was like going to the gilded Opera in Paris. Customers who really understood clothes went to Madame Grès. Nobody could drape like her, nobody could use jersey like her. Another Sphinx-like couturière with a seemingly ancient honed wisdom was Gabrielle 'Coco' Chanel. When the first pictures of Chanel's 1954 comeback collection came out in the press I was at Hammersmith and I didn't particularly like what I saw. It was not until I actually went to a Chanel show that I understood her particular magic – her chic, her craftsmanship, her style. I remember seeing her sitting at the top of the stairs smoking and looking on at everything and everyone below. And what a show!

I didn't realise she had these beautiful little shift dresses and stunning cocktail dresses. Chanel had the most beautiful models in Paris and the audience too was mesmerising – these were the most chic women in Paris. The whole show was riveting. Chanel always had these lovely little touches: a print blouse under a suit, with the jacket and skirt lined in the same print as the blouse; two seams in the front of a skirt cut to make it flip forward so it moved naturally with the wearer...

As students, we were equally interested in the new talent like Pierre Cardin, and Hubert de Givenchy, who had been an assistant to the couturière, Schiaparelli. Givenchy didn't have much money for his first collection so he designed it in cotton and organdie, making it very fresh and young. It was always very exciting for myself and the other students when up-and-coming young designers became newsworthy – it was what we aspired to.

These important visits to the Continental fashion shows continued under my next professor, Janey Ironside. Janey was very different indeed from Madge Garland, and had briefly been her assistant at the Royal College of Art before leaving to set up her own dressmaking business. When Madge Garland retired, Janey was invited back as her successor. Janey was from a younger generation, less intimidating than her predecessor but just as charismatic and, having been a dressmaker, she had a more hands-on approach to teaching. She made sure that we made maximum use of all the advantages that the Royal College had to offer. Significantly, she was part of, and understood, the new liberated direction that fashion was taking.

When she was appointed in 1956, fashion was already dramatically changing, and she encouraged us to change with it. In Paris, Dior and Balenciaga still reigned supreme, but there were newcomers – including Pierre Cardin and Guy Laroche, and a little later André Courrèges – who were emerging with quite revolutionary new looks. In London, Mary Quant had opened Bazaar, her cult boutique on the King's Road, and for the first time the pre-eminence of Parisian *haute couture* was being challenged by more youthful aspirations.

Janey had her own way of teaching for the outside world, and was very much in tune with all these shifts and the new influences that were emerging. They had an informality and a modernity that coincided with her own views on fashion. She became Principal of the Fashion School in my second year. It was the start of a time when she became instrumental in nurturing the careers of many important designers, including Sally Tuffin and Marion Foale, Ossie Clark and Bill Gibb.

I got to know Janey well on a student visit to Paris. The Fashion School had managed to forge links with the Chambre Syndicale de la Couture in Paris, enabling Janey to bring two students to couturiers' customer shows, which was a great privilege. At the time, there was intense security surrounding the unveiling of couture designs and any little infringement was seized upon to protect the integrity of the House and its potentially lucrative new season designs. In my third

28

year I was chosen to accompany Janey with fellow student Richard Lachlan, and was thrilled to find out we were going first to Dior. After the show we sat at a nearby café and made a few sketches from memory.

The next morning, Janey was called into the Chambre's press office. We had been spotted by a Dior insider doing our sketches and were accused of industrial espionage! Janey pleaded in her broken French that we were only students and hadn't even been sketching at the show. With the thought of the guillotine hanging over us, we were allowed to go. Of course none of this could dampen our enthusiasm for the shows, which were wonderfully glamorous affairs in sumptuous salons, where every detail was perfect – even the air was sprayed with the house scent for the ultimate couture experience. It was the antithesis of what had been for so long Britain's grim post-war austerity years and I was bowled over by the sheer luxury of it all.

Though I saw collections by Balenciaga, Chanel, Balmain, Jean Dessès, and Cardin, Dior always remained my favourite. French couture in the '50s was dominated by him. I have always admired his glamorous and elegant style and he remains a lasting influence on my work. When he died in 1957 it was the end of an era; his death was almost the nail in the coffin for French couture. It *would* survive, but never to reach the same heady heights. The world was changing and fashion had to reflect those changes.

The evolution of the new wave of fashion then sweeping through Europe can be traced in the history of the house of Dior. I was lucky enough to see not only the last Christian Dior collection, but also the first by his assistant Yves Saint Laurent for Dior – the whole world was waiting with bated breath. I also saw the first independent Yves Saint Laurent show for his own house. They were the three major influential shows of those years. These were exciting times – fashion was in flux – and the rules were about to be thrown out of the window.

In my third year, Joanne Brogden, who had been my teacher at Hammersmith, joined the Fashion School as Janey's assistant, and became one of my tutors again, much to my delight. In my early days at Hammersmith, Joanne had been very supportive and was extremely proud of me when I won my precious Royal College place. I was pleased to be able to have her guidance once again, and she became a good friend after I graduated.

At last it was time for me to show what I had learned – the climax of my studies came as I prepared to present my final year collection at the Royal College fashion show in June 1958. Each student had a minimum of six outfits in the show, mine were all evening dresses. I had no real interest in tailoring or little day dresses, I just wanted to do glamour. I can remember fitting my dresses in Janey's office for her approval, and I tried to emulate as best I could the glamour that I had experienced in the Paris and Italian salons.

This was the time when another powerful woman – who was to become the most important influence in my career – entered my life. Belinda Bellville, the society dressmaker to debutantes and duchesses, came to see my final year show and offered me a job as an assistant designer. She was starting to make a name for herself with her small Belgravia company, which she had set up in 1953. Now pregnant with her second child, she was looking for a designer to help with the collections, and she liked my work.

Fortune was smiling on me. The meeting with Belinda was the turning point, and from that moment, I was on my way. This was the beginning of a wonderful partnership between Belinda and myself, which would last twenty-five years.

OPPOSITE PAGE It was glamour all the way for my final year Royal College graduation show. Seen here, fitting a dress in Janey Ironside's office, 1958

31

BELTING ALONG WITH BELLVILLE

'BELTING ALONG WITH BELLVILLE'[1] I joined Bellville et Cie in 1958, the year the last debutante was presented at court. It was a very exciting time to be a fledgling designer. In Paris, couture was reeling from the loss of Christian Dior, who had died the year before, and his talented young assistant, Yves Saint Laurent had taken up the reins with a very different approach. There were also stirrings from a raft of new wave designers. In London, Mary Quant was revolutionising fashion from the streets up, having opened her cult boutique, Bazaar on the King's Road in 1955. The whole mood of the country was changing; the grim post–war years were left behind as Britain experienced a new era of plenty. Harold Macmillan, who had just succeeded Anthony Eden as prime minister, summed up the new burgeoning consumerism by telling us all, "You've never had it so good".

In the midst of all this I arrived at Bellville to start my first job as assistant designer, and I immediately saw how vital the aristocracy and their debutante daughters were to Belinda's small dressmaking business. The debutantes and the era they represented were all part and parcel of the formality and convention that defined '50s Britain. It was an intensely hierarchical and class-conscious time. My designing career began in the rarefied world of couture and, in terms of customers, it was all about society and 'doing' the London Season. The rich and the British aristocracy have a history of having dresses made for them. Their daughters were traditionally, and expensively, launched into society and were formally presented to the reigning monarch at Buckingham Palace in a ceremony that dated back to George III's reign. After this, the main focus of the debutante was a series of lunches, cocktail parties, and most importantly 'coming out' balls, all aimed at developing and reinforcing their social credentials and connections, and ultimately finding them a suitable husband. It was all endless parties, ambitious parents, and girls in white gloves denoting a pristine character, certified by no less a figure than the Lord Chamberlain.

This concentrated calendar of dedicated partying demanded a sophisticated and glamorous wardrobe, and Belinda, who had been a deb herself, spotted a gap in the market for young, pretty debutante dresses that were also exclusive. Several hundred girls all going to the same dances for the three months of the Season was a ready-made clientele, and a ready-to-wear dress no matter how pretty or reasonably priced lost its charm when three or four girls turned up in the same one. Debutantes came to Bellville for something different, something that they wouldn't meet another deb wearing, and Belinda was soon hailed as the "Debs' darling" designer.

In the magazines and newspapers debutantes made the headlines, alongside society figures and elegant models, as the pin-ups of the day. They were young, stylish and beautiful and many of them were wearing Bellville et Cie. It was the era of the 'celebutante' and the title 'Deb of the Year' was a hotly contested one; previous holders included the 1957 winner, the exquisite Henrietta Tiarks, who first wore Bellville as a debutante, and who continued to wear the label when she became the Marchioness of Tavistock. Even when the Palace presentations ended and the press predicted that the day of the deb was over, the 'coming out' parties and balls continued and there was no lack of business for Bellville.

Belinda Bellville had set up her small dressmaking business in Belgravia in 1953. She had great taste and style, but no formal design training. However, she did have fashion in her blood: her grandmother, Mrs Gordon Leith, known as 'Cuckoo' Leith, was a society woman who had run a noted dressmaking business in the '20s at Sheridan House in London's Savile Row. During the Second World War the building was bombed and was eventually taken over by a young couturier at the start of his illustrious career – none other than Hardy Amies.

OPPOSITE PAGE In my element: working with Belinda Bellville at Cadogan Lane, where according to *Women's Wear Daily* we designed for 'London's young...London's rich...London's beautiful' [*Women's Wear Daily*, 25 May, 1967. Photograph by John Young, 1962] OVERLEAF LEFT Pat O'Reilly, one of the top models of the day, wears a short evening dress in pink moiré taffeta at a Bellville show in 1960. The salon was so full that the crowd overflowed onto the stairs OVERLEAF RIGHT Society beauty and Bellville client, Lady Beatty, married to one of the wealthiest men in England, models for Bellville in a strapless taffeta and lace ballgown

Belinda was the tall and striking daughter of the Hon. Mrs Peter Pleydell-Bouverie. After Belinda 'came out' as a 'deb' and was launched into society she had a succession of jobs in London. At nineteen she worked in a Bond Street dress shop, closely followed by stints as a fashion journalist and then as assistant to fashion photographer, Keith Ewart. Through these various jobs she gained invaluable practical experience and contacts – the perfect launch-pad for her own fashion business. In her early twenties, on her marriage to financier David Whately, Belinda gave up working, but found that "after I'd been married a bit I wanted something to do. And what I wanted to do was make pretty dresses, the sort of thing I wanted to wear myself but couldn't find.": At just half an inch under six feet tall, Belinda cut an elegant and willowy figure, but she was frustrated that she couldn't find chic, well-made clothes to fit her tall frame or match her personal style. In the early '50s, 'good' clothes were generally too old and matronly to appeal to her young taste. So she determined to design her own. In the street one day she met Mrs Sydna Scott who was on the verge of giving up her small dressmaking company in Kinnerton Street, Belgravia and Belinda immediately jumped at the chance of joining forces with her. With her husband's blessing, Belinda sold the car her brother had given them as a wedding present and put the £500 into the business as their only start-up capital, and the new company was formed. Astonishingly, it remains the only capital the company has ever needed – to this day we have never had a loan, an overdraft, or any outside money. From these small beginnings the company has been totally self-financing and self-perpetuating, a great testament to its consistent success. Thanks to Belinda's husband, David Whately, the company was put on a financially secure route from the outset; he invested the money in gold shares, which proved to be a very sound investment, and generally guided our financial interests.

Starting out as Bellville et Cie (Bellville & Co.), it was symptomatic of the times that Belinda gave the company this title in the belief that it would add a touch of French atmosphere and prestige to the label. After all, fashion direction then came almost exclusively from the Parisian *haute couture* designers, and French dresses were equated with instant appeal and luxury. She later regretted the 'et Cie', "It's the sort of thing you think is chic when you're young," she told Ernestine Carter, fashion editor of the *Sunday Times* in 1964. Right from the start, demand outstripped what the "thimble-sized" Kinnerton Street premises could supply. The £500 had provided two rooms, one sewing machine and two seamstresses. Space, staff and facilities were all at a premium. While 'Scottie', as Sydna Scott was affectionately known, mainly sold in their shop (which took up one of the two rooms), Belinda came up with the designs and was often reduced to dreaming up her dresses in an unconventional setting. "In the early days when we only had two tiny rooms," she revealed, "I used to go and design in the pub next door!"

Nevertheless, Belinda had aspirations to create a proper English couture house and was determined to make quality clothes in a younger style. The response to the first customer shows, which took place in her grandmother's elegant drawing room in Manchester Square, W1, was, to Belinda's surprise, astonishing, "It's one thing to invite your friends, but quite another when they come back and place orders. The place was bursting and half of them couldn't get in. I think we succeeded because the ideas were so fresh." Rolls Royces and Bentleys were parked bumper to bumper around the Square with customers eager to see and order a fresh, new brand of British couture.

Belinda's own background as a former debutante gave her a social entrée to her future customers, who were largely drawn from three groups of women: debutantes and their mothers; the young-marrieds, like Belinda herself, who wanted quality clothes but with a sense of modern

verve and style; and traditional couture customers who wanted to be dressed by the new London name. It was definitely a society clientele that gravitated to the label's new style. No wonder the press called her, 'Belinda Bellville, the top people's darling', and that the company was lauded for making 'the chic-est, prettiest evening dresses'.[6] The business soon outgrew the original premises and in 1957 Belinda and Mrs Scott moved to 14 Motcomb Street, Belgravia. By the next year, Belinda was pregnant with her second child and went to the Royal College of Art show to look for someone to assist her. This was the moment when my life in fashion really began.

From the day I started I was thrown in at the deep end: I sold, I sewed, I sketched designs and drew them up for customers, I made toiles. We were a tiny team, only about ten people, and everybody just did everything. There was always a lot going on: choosing fabrics, doing fittings, checking the workrooms, and it was a big learning curve. In Motcomb Street Belinda had the whole building: the ground floor housed the showroom and right at the back of this there was a 'cupboard' for me to design in; the first and second floors contained the dressmaking workrooms where I would drape and pin lengths of fabric directly onto Belinda to get the shapes for the collections. Perhaps Belinda was her own best model – just as well as we didn't have a house model then. I liked the fact that Belinda was so tall, it meant I could work out quite exaggerated shapes and she was an inspiring mannequin – she had very good legs and she was a glamorous and attractive woman.

Everything moved up another gear after I arrived. When I started it was a little dressmaking company, then the business really started to take off. We expanded and had a tailoring workroom in Wilton Place and were forced to take on additional space in Motcomb Street so that we had two premises there, one on either side of the street; we fitted the clothes in one and had the shop in the other. As one newspaper reported, 'Belinda Bellville's boutiques are on each side of a small and charming street so that one often sees famous clients trotting across the footpath followed by an assistant carrying a model dress.'[7]

At my first Bellville shows in the late '50s, I was thrilled about the models who would be wearing our designs. It was a roll call of some of the biggest names in modelling at that time – among them Bronwen Pugh, who modelled for Balmain and Anne Gunning who modelled for Chanel. Later there was Christine Tidmarsh who had modelled for Dior and then followed Yves Saint Laurent when he opened his own couture house. Some of our models were 'celebutantes' like Lady Beatty, and many married into the aristocracy, as she had done. Bronwen Pugh married Lord Astor, Fiona Campbell-Walter married Baron von Thyssen and Sevilla Glass-Hooper became the Princess Sevilla Hercolani. Modelling had become a reputable profession for a girl with the right look – and that look was all haughty sophistication and an immaculate 'don't touch' perfection, quite different to how the models of the '60s would look. To complement our dresses we borrowed precious jewellery from Cartier. Our show venues were equally impressive. We hired or borrowed suitably grand premises – I remember one of the earliest of my Bellville shows was held at the aristocratic Londonderry House at 65 Park Lane, while another was held at Claus von Bulow's apartment in Belgrave Square.

Nadia.

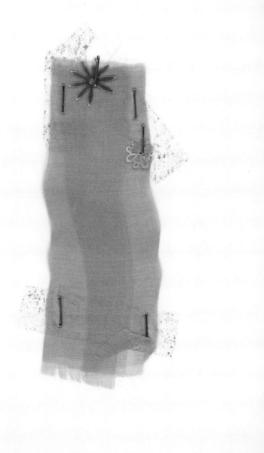

Candida

44

Belinda intended to develop her dressmaking business into a proper couture business – and that's where I came in. I brought with me all the training and skills I had acquired at the Royal College of Art. What was particularly appealing when I went to Bellville was that Belinda had an obsession with period costume and loved romantic dresses, so we were very similar in our influences. We each brought something different to the company, and we also brought out the best in each other. My expertise and enthusiasm perfectly complemented Belinda's intuitive flair, and together we shared a love of colour and sumptuous fabrics. We were, I suppose, a perfect double act. I was yang to Belinda's yin. I grew with Belinda and she grew with me.

The company expanded enormously under the two of us. I was very much recognised as being a young ex-Royal College of Art designer. Gradually we developed as couturiers doing our own thing – and expanded into a full-blown couture house equal to any of the leading London couturiers, who were all members of the Incorporated Society. We were assiduously courted by the Incorporated Society, and we were flattered, but we firmly turned down the invitations to join their ranks, even though they were keen for new blood. We were part of the '60s scene, we looked at designers like Mary Quant and felt that ready-to-wear was the way forward, and we soon added this string to our bow. They were very exciting years – everything was new and progressive, just like us.

The aesthetic we forged together – a new style of British couture that was young, fresh and exciting – perfectly mirrored the times in which we were working and living. It offered a new glamorous, up-to-the-minute alternative to the more traditional conservatism of the Incorporated Society of London Fashion Designers, who were making very proper, English county clothes for the most part. Our clothes were still very couture, and to begin with they were slightly less expensive than the other London couturiers. While we surged ahead, their fortunes were on the wane. By the mid-sixties the original number of Incorporated Society designers had almost halved from eleven to just seven. Belinda and I did not consider ourselves part of the Establishment. We were consciously doing something new: keeping the polished finish and luxurious workmanship of couture, but giving our designs a fresh, new, modern take. This was our hallmark and what distinguished us from any of the other London couturiers. At the time, there was nobody else doing what we were doing. We were getting plenty of press coverage, as well as customers eager for our elegant, romantic clothes. Not only were we doing young couture, we were equally successful with our 'new guard' ready-to-wear.

Bellville was the label of the Young Set, who wanted made-to-measure dresses at affordable prices. We tapped into a need for well-cut, well-made, flattering clothes for a fashion-forward, moneyed set who wanted couture, but not in a stiff, stuffy way. They wanted their clothes to be high quality and high fashion in terms of trends. It was the art of clothes to get you noticed. The season's most lavish coming-out parties, the year's most high-powered balls, society's best-connected weddings were not complete without starring dresses by Bellville. In 1966, when

London was truly swinging, *The Times* was singing our praises, 'In this country the most successful couturier is Bellville. The clothes from this house are completely right and eminently suited for the better end, as one might say, of the English social scene. They know to within an inch how much décolletage the duchess will stand at dinner, and that Cheltenham racecourse is a draughty place. Bellville customers will wear diamond brooches in their lapels and shocking pink is always a good selling colour as it looks so well against a Bermuda tan. The Bellville collection answers all their needs to perfection, and is the most covetable and wearable you can imagine, and in impeccable taste for England (which is what the American buyers want). And it sells. At the end of the shows, the customers flock to put down orders as though it were bargain day at Barkers.'[8]

London's fashion scene was being played out in two places simultaneously. It was not just Chelsea that set the swinging tone in '60s London. There was another, different fashion dynamic at work – and it was taking place in upmarket Belgravia. Just as Mary Quant designs and the 'youthquake' had ushered in a new era and a new order in ready-to-wear centred in Chelsea – not to mention John Stephens in Carnaby Street and Biba in Kensington – so Bellville did the same for British couture in Belgravia. Belgravia was home to a younger brand of couture, and home to many of those who wore it, '...the young élégantes for whom money is no option,' as *Harpers & Queen* described our clientele.[9] This was a more *soigné* style of fashion, but still adventurous. While newspapers hailed the miniskirt and the 'Biba babe', on our side of London we had overflowing order books, an influential clientele and we were hailed with equal enthusiasm by the press, buyers and customers on both sides of the Atlantic.

Interestingly, this duality at the forefront of London's '60s fashion scene – Chelsea versus Belgravia – was thrown up by contemporary press features, as well as the choices for the two designers whose collections would be showcased at the prestigious 1963 Berkeley Debutantes Dress Show: Mary Quant and Bellville. I do think the '60s were a very exciting time to be a designer. Things were changing so much after Dior died. The traditional English couture houses all but fizzled out and new designers like Mary Quant, Tuffin and Foale, Ossie Clark, Jean Muir, John Bates and Gerald McCann challenged and changed the whole mood of fashion. Bellville bridged the gap between the Establishment and the new wave designers. We were also different in that we were doing couture and ready-to-wear equally successfully – designers like Quant and Muir were not couturiers.

Everyone wanted the 'London Look'; the swinging '60s were all about the London scene, and something else that was focused on London was the boutique look – boutiques offering up-to-the-minute ready-to-wear outfits. It happened gradually and yet it seemed it was overnight that everything changed for us. Five years after I arrived, we needed bigger premises to satisfy the increasing demand for our collections and in 1963 we moved into exciting new premises in Cadogan Lane, Belgravia. At that time couturiers salons were all crystal chandeliers and draped silk curtains, but that was not for us. Belinda converted an old stable off Sloane Street into a large showroom with workrooms above. It was a blend of bohemian and grand – that's what made it modern. There were whitewashed brick walls, old wooden beams, and rush matting on the floors and Belinda filled it with an eclectic collection of antiques. It was described as 'the most unusual salon in London'.[10] It seemed that the whole world wanted to come and see what we were doing. Mrs Evangeline Bruce, wife of the American Ambassador, described by *Harper's Bazaar* as one of the world's most influential style-setters, brought Jackie Kennedy and her sister Princess Lee Radziwill. Pamela Colin, a *Vogue* fashion editor who later became Lady Harlech, brought

OPPOSITE PAGE *Life* magazine's iconic image of London designers put me in the frame with such names as Mary Quant, Jean Muir, Sally Tuffin and Marion Foale under the title, 'Brash new breed of British Designers'. According to *Life*, we were 'out to shake up traditional British fashion' and had already become 'a major style influence in England' [Photograph Norman Parkinson © The Norman Parkinson Archive] OVERLEAF Two of the typically glamorous Bellville et Cie evening dresses modelled by Bronwen Pugh (who later became Lady Astor), 1959, photographed by Michel Molinare

Jennifer's Diary and always made sure that Jennifer (better known as Betty Kenward, the arbiter and legendary chronicler of all things to do with high society) had a good seat at our shows, as she always reported on our socially élite clientele. Belinda did not like the newspapers and would often turn down interviews. She had an absolute horror of papers that she called "the tuppenny bloods", and wouldn't let certain titles through the door.

Belinda could be grand, but she could be very friendly and down to earth and she did have a great sense of humour. She was a bit strict, a bit 'jolly hockey sticks', and a bit of a headmistress at heart. Belinda was the biggest influence on my life: in taste, interests, and lifestyle. I was very in awe of her as she was a very strong character. Nearly six feet tall with long, slender legs and a very determined personality, everything about Belinda was big: she had a big personality and big ideas. Nor did she suffer fools gladly. Belinda had great enthusiasm and was very inspired and inspiring when she liked something, but if she didn't like a dress, you would know it! In the early days Belinda had the problem of trying to balance a husband and three children with a demanding career, and because of this more and more responsibility for running the company would end up on my shoulders. By the time we had moved to Cadogan Lane, Belinda had stopped working full-time, and was coming in just three days a week and then spending a long weekend in the country.

We were very different, but the thing that drew us together was a great love of colour and beautiful fabrics. Both of us shared a slightly bohemian streak. My Middle Eastern background came out in my preference for colour and adornment and decoration. Belinda was more restrained, but she was very good on colour and fabric – and I learned that from her. We always chose materials together, using the most luxurious from the very best couture fabric houses. Designing in the '60s and '70s was all about tapping into the youth cult – that sense of exuberance and experimentation. Other British couturiers seemed to be frightened of colour, whereas for us it was fundamental, it was one of the things that really set us apart. We were always very bold in our use of colour and print, and to this end, in the early '60s when Belinda and I were looking for someone to design exclusive prints for us, we set up a meeting with Celia Birtwell. She was heavily pregnant at the time and had to cancel, so we approached Zandra Rhodes instead. Zandra and I struck up an instant rapport and we have been best friends ever since.

Belinda had a magpie's eye, a genuine love of beautiful, special things. She would pull out of her handbag a tiny piece of something – ribbon, a bit of embroidery – and say, "Look at this, it's such a wonderful colour, we should do something like this in the collection." There was always something quirky about Belinda which was still totally in keeping with her good taste. She would sweep into work, and then sweep out again, leaving destruction in her wake. She always gave me the impression that she thought five maids were scampering after her to deal with the fallout! She was an Aries and came and went in a flurry of spontaneous energy and activity. I was a calm Libran who wanted peace and harmony and order.

Together, Belinda and I were a consummate success story, but we were very different, not only in nature but in looks, and this wasn't lost on the press. In a feature entitled 'Britons of Belgravia', *America's Women's Wear Daily* painted the following picture: 'Belinda Bellville is tall, blonde, slender with aristocratic good looks. Her whippet, Albemarle, matches her in slender elegance. Her co-designer, David Sassoon, is dark and exotic.'[12] In London, Ernestine Carter also highlighted this contrast in her *Sunday Times* feature: 'The long (Miss Bellville just under six feet) and the short (Mr Sassoon of Napoleonic height) of it is that the firm is belting along from success to success.'[13]

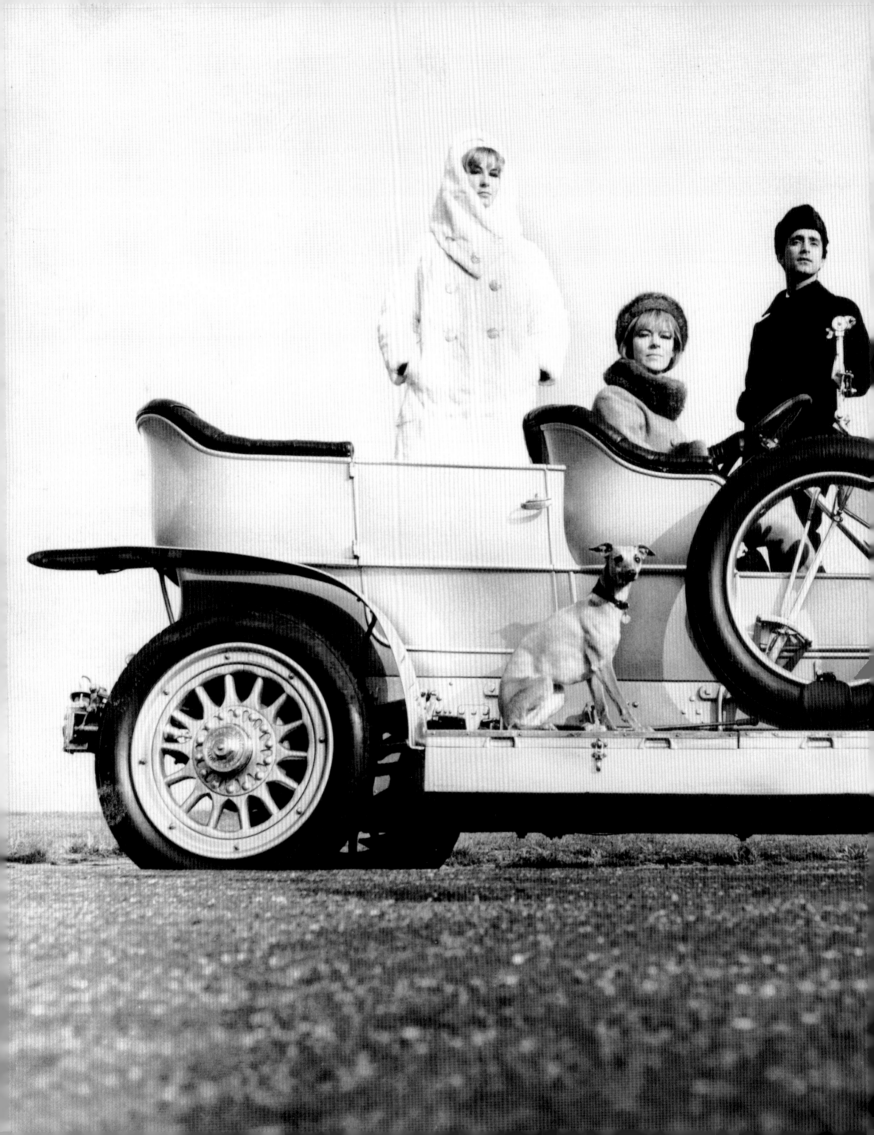

SIGNS OF THE TIMES- BELLVILLE SASSOON THROUGH THE DECADES

THIS PAGE Psychedelic dress, 1969 OPPOSITE PAGE Model Jill Kennington strikes a pose in Bellville's paisley hooded dress, photographed by John Cowan at Westminster Bridge for the cover of *Queen*, the top-selling magazine of the '60s [*Queen*, 4 December, 1962. © The National Magazine Company] OVERLEAF LEFT *Harper's Bazaar* acclaims the leaders of the International Look: 'Bellville's cobweb of crystals and beads worn over white chiffon culottes cut to hang like a skirt' [*Harper's Bazaar*, May 1964. Photograph Terence Donovan. © The National Magazine Company] OVERLEAF RIGHT Evening dress in shifting layers of print and colour worn with space-age helmet in pink plastic [*Harper's Bazaar*, May 1966. Photograph David Montgomery. © The National Magazine Company]

SIGNS OF THE TIMES — BELLVILLE SASSOON THROUGH THE DECADES

1960s

When I joined Bellville in 1958, London had already started to set the fashion pendulum swinging to its own beat. The seeds of the '60s were 'sewn' in the '50s – the design students of the '50s, like me, became the designers of the '60s and we were alive to all the new possibilities, new opportunities, new moods, new inspirations, and more than willing to make of them what we could. I couldn't have been in a better place – London was where it was at. All the rules were broken. The new mantra was "anything goes" and it did.

In the '50s daughters had aspired to look like their sophisticated mothers; in the '60s the roles were reversed – everyone wanted to look young and mothers were as keen as their daughters to emulate the new modern street fashions. Where conformity had been the watchword of the '50s, now individuality was the thing, and those whose looks were unusual and unconventional became the new style icons, like the coltish young models Jean Shrimpton, Penelope Tree and the face of '66, Twiggy.

As the decade unfolded, with it came the youth revolution and fashion was its epicentre. Inspiration came from the new music scene, the new breed of artists, writers, playwrights and the exploding creativity of its youth. All the arts were undergoing a period of accelerated creativity. Fashion photography also changed to reflect this. It was the birth of the era of the personality: the fashion photographers were personalities and the models were personalities. The starring names were Jean Shrimpton, Celia Hammond, Jill Kennington, Marisa Berenson, Penelope Tree, Twiggy and Veruschka; and the star-makers were David Bailey, Norman Parkinson, Terence Donovan, Justin de Villeneuve, David Montgomery, Barry Lategan and Clive Arrowsmith. Even actresses like Faye Dunaway and Julie Christie got in on the modelling act.

London defined the new era. When the legendary editor of American *Vogue*, Diana Vreeland, announced, 'The British are Coming!'[14] she was referring to David Bailey and Jean Shrimpton, two of the most potent image makers in the '60s, but she could just as easily have been referring to the London look as a whole. And 'Swinging London' got the world swinging; the 'London Look' was in demand internationally. America looked across the Atlantic to the London scene and was swept up in the creative fashion explosion. Visiting Americans made a bee-line for our Cadogan Lane shop, and then went off to buy antiques at Portobello. Norman Parkinson was commissioned by *Life* magazine to photograph London's leading designers – and I became part of the famous Chelsea Embankment photo shoot, alongside such stellar names as Mary Quant and Jean Muir.[15]

Fashion-wise the '60s was all about the boutique look – something London had that nowhere else had at that time. A group of highly individual fashion entrepreneurs seized the moment and became an integral part of the scene: Quant's Bazaar and Ginger Group collections in the King's Road, John Stephens in Carnaby Street, Barbara Hulanicki's Biba in Kensington. After Candice Bergen came in to see us, I remember taking her shopping in the boutiques in the King's Road to show her all the new trend shops. Even Saint Laurent came to soak up the atmosphere of the King's Road and translated what he saw into his next collections. London's

64

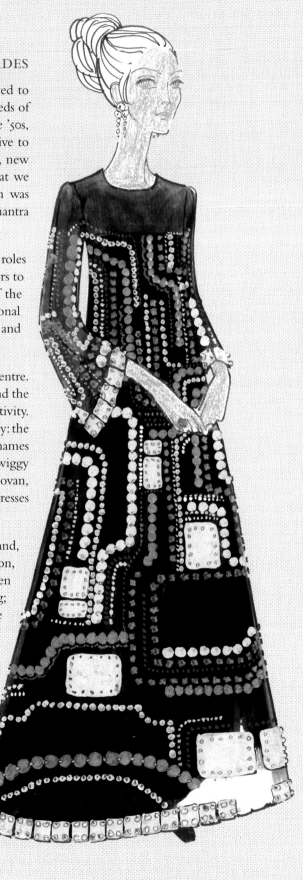

QUEEN 2/-
DECEMBER 4th 1962

MONUMENTAL
Ideas about:
CHRISTMAS PRESENTS
CLOTHES
PEOPLE

ALBA.

scene had a direct effect on the Parisian couture and traditional houses like Lanvin, Jean Dessès and Jacques Heim were replaced by Yves Saint Laurent, Cardin, and Courrèges. London was the place to be, and as a designer working in the middle of this tumultuous cultural explosion, I felt in my element.

Our salon at Cadogan Lane epitomised it all – we were daring, we were different. There, and at our next salon in Sloane Street, we became more experimental – reflecting the mood of the times. Belinda could see the direction we needed to go. She let me have my head, let me have my fling, and it was the right way to go. I was more arty, more *outré* than Belinda. She was Establishment and I was anti-Establishment. At Bellville we had the look of the moment – the minidresses and psychedelic prints, but we interpreted them as couture, for a clientele who still expected quality. The look on the high street was cheap and inexpensive to keep pace with the demand for constant change. At Bellville the '60s look moved upmarket with embroidered gold mesh minidresses and lavish lace-trimmed culottes. What Bellville brought to the contemporary scene was real star glamour – combining contemporary trends and novelty with couture.

Five years after I joined Bellville, in 1963 we launched our ready-to-wear Boutique collection, and Belinda made me a director and partner. In 1965 we came to the attention of Vogue Patterns, who snapped us up for their pattern books, and started a successful partnership that continues today. Our profile was rapidly changing and our reputation for designing for debutantes was left behind, although our reputation for quality was not.

In July 1965 *Women's Wear Daily* devoted a full page to Bellville under the headline, 'Britons of Belgravia – The British are still coming. This time it is Bellville who has invaded the American fashion shore. They are of the English school. Their look is well bred, with equal emphasis on quality, exciting fabrics and creativity.'[16]

Bellville's most successful years coincided with this era, when London's influence was truly international. And the press were very supportive. Beatrix Miller, the then editor of British *Vogue*, was renowned for promoting the best of British fashion at a time when it was spearheading the fashion revolution. As both couturiers and ready-to-wear designers we were ideally placed to take advantage of this, and she was a wonderful champion of our collections, as was her fashion editor, Melanie Miller, who used to ring up almost every week to call things in or commission something special for one of her shoots.

We took the success in our stride – frequent *Vogue* covers, editorials in the glossy fashion magazines every month, interviews, designing for Audrey Hepburn and Dusty Springfield, seeing our designs worn by Jean Shrimpton, Marisa Berenson and Penelope Tree photographed by Bailey. There would be a buzz in the workroom when someone – a royal or a VIP – was in, or as in the case of Peter Sellers, waiting outside for his wife Miranda Sellers, and later Britt Ekland, who was photographed wearing our Liberty print dress in *Vogue*.[17]

In the '60s all hell was let loose, it was a decade of creative decadence, a time of excess and exuberance, optimism and outrageousness. However, this world of youth culture and

ARABELLA.

A BEVY of enchanting dresses for a summer's night, designed by Belinda Belville for, from left, Lady Anne Tennant, Viscountess Cranborne, Lady Pamela Hicks and Lady Porchester.

Dressing for the Dance of the Year

FABULOUS JEWELS will come out of storage on Friday for the party of the year. Nine hundred guests—among them the Queen, Prince Philip and Princess Margaret—will drive to Luton Hoo, the home of Lady Zia Wernher, for the coming out of her granddaughter, 18-year-old Alexandra Phillips. Belinda Belville designed the bevy of enchanting dresses, sketched above, that some of the guests will wear as they drift round the great, cool gardens on a summer's night. Lady Anne Tennant will stand out in white organza frosted with crystals and pearls. Viscountess Cranborne has chosen dark green organza topped with a froth of white organdie, Lady Pamela Hicks, a Princess dress of shocking pink faille with a bodice of drifting ostrich feathers. Lady Porchester chose a sheath dress of maize-coloured crêpe with a bodice of white lace.

Sketch and report by BERYL HARTLAND

69

Belles of the Ball: THIS PAGE Bellville's designs for 'The Party of the Year' as featured by Beryl Hartland in the *Daily Telegraph*, 1964

nightclubbing was not for Belinda. She was on the periphery of the 1960s, she was never really a part of it in that way. She moved in much higher echelons; and counted amongst her friends people like Princess Alexandra. Belinda led a much more traditional society life, with a husband, three children and two houses to look after.

In contrast, I was young and single and I embraced the hedonism and self-expression that characterised the decade, and released my inner self. I fully immersed myself in the '60s. It just felt like my time. In the '50s I had aspired to look like a mature designer and wore suits; but all that changed in the '60s, when my conformist attitude went right out of the window. Now I bought my clothes at shops like Mr Freedom, Biba, and Granny Takes a Trip, and shopped in Carnaby Street. I lived in Chelsea in a flat in Draycott Place, just off the King's Road. On Saturday afternoons I loved to get dressed up in the latest trends and walk up and down the King's Road with my friends looking at what everyone else was wearing. It was a kaleidoscope of colour and exhibitionism and we all loved being part of the show.

I liked to be outrageous. I used to put a rose transfer on my face, which I wore even for work. Princess Alexandra gave Belinda a cow-bell from one of her Indian travels, which Belinda gave to me and I wore it round my neck! When I did wear a suit it wasn't a conventional one. I remember I had a suit in bottle green velvet, which I wore with a purple print georgette shirt. With another velvet suit I always wore a waistcoat, but I changed the buttons so they were antique cut steel. I had shirts from Biba with long fringeing and beads hanging down. I was influenced by the musical *Hair* and grew my hair so that it was almost an Afro look. When we had parties my hairdresser used to thread flowers through my hair.

I had an unfortunate start when I met one of our great press champions, Ernestine Carter of the *Sunday Times*. She came in for an outfit to wear to an awards ceremony and it fell to me to help her. I was so nervous that when I zipped up her dress I got my Mr Fish kipper tie well and truly caught. I started to pull back and she started to pull forward, and in the process she was choking me. I kept stuttering, "Oh, Miss Carter!" between gasped breaths, and in the end someone had to cut off my precious tie!

In the late '60s fashion was very decorative. Saint Laurent was a big influence and so was Kenzo. Like them, Belinda loved ethnic prints and beading, and she enjoyed mixing these elements, print on print, colour on colour. She would wear wonderful gipsy looks – a black velvet jacket over a multicoloured skirt and boots. She would sweep in wearing capes and had a particularly memorable big blanket cape, black with red crocodiles woven into it – very dashing and dramatic, but always elegant with an edge – that was Belinda.

When I came to Bellville I introduced the idea of themed collections as a way of making the designs come together as a look. The themes sometimes came from my travels. There was a Spanish collection, then Arabian, Chinese, Mexican, Indian. There were flamenco-style ruffles, and Inca-inspired embroideries from my trip to Mexico. These were our versions of fantasy fashion: Scheherazade dresses, Cossack satin tunics, jewelled bras and printed harem pants. Our designs could be exotic and extravagant, but they were also chic and elegant. What really zings out from the pages of *Vogue* and all the other glossy magazines in which we were featured was COLOUR!

The '60s was a time of huge changes in the world of fashion. I loved the new freedom of dress for men and women and 'flower power' added a new dimension to the world of fashion, music and the arts. This influence changed forever the way we dressed and behaved and it was reflected in the collections Belinda and I put together. I think it was possibly the most exciting and creative period in the history of the company. I look back at the '60s as a great adventure, every day seemed to have some excitement which encouraged one to break new ground in design.

THIS PAGE Eastern Promise: 'jewelled bra and wide pleated pants so tremendous they can be wafted around like butterfly wings' OPPOSITE PAGE In Demand: jewelled bra with printed chiffon sarong skirt, [*Queen*, 14-27 May, 1969. Photographs Clive Arrowsmith. © The National Magazine Company]

La Goulue.

Boucher.

THIS PAGE AND OPPOSITE PAGE 'Flowering fairy tale organdie', lace blouse and dirndl skirt appliquéd with summer posies, matching flower-strewn shoes [*Vogue*, June 1968. Photograph David Montgomery/*Vogue*. © The Condé Nast Publications Ltd] OVERLEAF Two Bellville trademarks: vivid colour and lavish embroidery LEFT 'sunshine chiffon scattered with sequin flowers' [*Vogue*, June 1967. Photograph David Bailey/*Vogue*. © The Condé Nast Publications Ltd], and RIGHT Bellville's individual way with 'jewel encrusted' embroidery became a typical hallmark. Bejewelled bodice and tinkling cuffs [*Vogue*, December 1968. Photograph Susan Wood/*Vogue*. © The Condé Nast Publications Ltd]

Ethnic meets Eastern OPPOSITE PAGE Lady Londonderry relaxes in an exuberantly printed silk georgette dress and matching cardigan embroidered with gold sequins [*Harpers & Queen*, December 1974. Photograph Eva Sereny/*Harpers & Queen*. © The National Magazine Company] THIS PAGE One of the traditional Qajar dynasty paintings from my personal collection, purchased in the '70s. Highly decorative and intricately painted, these jewel-like portraits of dancers and jugglers, commoners and kings, used to hang in the 18th-century harems and coffee houses of Persia, and remain evocative and inspirational images.

97

A tale of romance: the period details of the *belle époque* reworked for the nostalgic Seventies OVERLEAF LEFT Romantic details, pin-tucked dress with lace inserts, plumed hat and parasol [*Vogue*, June 1974. Photograph Toscani/*Vogue*. © The Condé Nast Publications Ltd] OVERLEAF RIGHT Proust revisited an extravagance of fine pleating in silk paper taffeta, tiered dress with caped bodice, peplum waist and full skirt, matching plumed taffeta hat [*Vogue*, December 1971. Photograph Christa Peters/*Vogue*. © The Condé Nast Publications Ltd]

in *Vogue* and caught Lady Lambton's eye.[18] She commissioned one with a scene of her country house – with handpainted boots to match!

One of the key looks of the '70s was the caftan. Many of Bellville Sassoon's glamorous versions were featured in *Vogue* and *Harper's Bazaar*, and because of this we were asked to dress Elizabeth Taylor for her 1972 film, *Zee and Company*, in which she played a fashion designer. Most actresses I've dressed have been quite normal and natural, but Elizabeth Taylor was quite the diva. When we went to see her on the set she kept us waiting for two-and-a-half hours. We were there to fit a bright, multicoloured caftan dress, a style that would become something of a Taylor trademark. It was the day after her husband, now Sir Richard Burton, had been invested, and when La Taylor eventually appeared she was wearing the famous Krupp diamond ring. While we were doing the fitting, my fitter kept inclining her head and eyebrows towards the finger that wore the ring. Halfway through the fitting Elizabeth Taylor's son came in wanting to borrow her car. "Mum," he said "can I take the Rolls?" Elizabeth was all smiles. "Of course darling, which one – the white or the black?"

ABOVE AND OPPOSITE PAGE The 3-piece outfit for Elizabeth Taylor's 1972 film, *Zee and Company*; an ethnic-inspired caftan in a Bernard Nevill Liberty print with tasselled bell sleeves and hood, worn over a tunic and matching knickerbockers

Another of the celebrities we dressed at this time was the film star Ava Gardner. Regarded by many as the most beautiful woman in the world, she could have been a diva, but wasn't. A regular at our couture shows, she loved soft, draped chiffon dresses. When Sinatra was due to play a series of concerts in London she came in to order a whole wardrobe. My fitter, Joan used to go to her London flat. Ava Gardner would rush back from the film set and before she did anything else, would take off her make-up – she looked just as beautiful without it. When the fitting was over she used to curl up in an armchair, "Right," she'd say, "Let's have an old fashioned", and she would pour Joan a whole tumbler full of bourbon. She used to like to chat and Joan wouldn't get out of there till 9.30 at night. One evening, the conversation got round to art and Ava Gardner insisted on lending Joan an impressive book on van Gogh. When Joan got home and opened it, inscribed on the flyleaf was the following handwritten dedication from one of Ava Gardner's admirers: 'This guy cut off his ear for love – god knows what I'd cut off for you!'

The '70s was a time of fantasy, fancy dress and escapist fashion, as epitomised by the contemporary musical genres – glam rock, disco and punk – perhaps to blot out the reality of inflation and strikes. The decade began with the three-day week and ended with the 'Winter of Discontent'. I can remember the staff in the workrooms having to work by candlelight as the electric machines and the irons came to a standstill – times were quite difficult. It was the era of glam rock and bohemian luxe as ethnic looks, folk art and folk costume became the defining influences. There was also a pastoral romanticism which carried over from the late '60s, and was influenced by Laura Ashley's nostalgic reinterpretations of Victoriana and Edwardiana.

Travelling with seventy dresses in garment bags the size of a wardrobe is a very precarious business. Customs, carousels, cars and 'planes all make it very stressful, as I found to my cost when I took my collection to New York in April 1978. This dramatic event came to be known as 'The Great American Disaster'. I was part of a group of fifteen British designers participating in a prestigious trade show, culminating in a gala fashion show in the presence of the British Ambassador. Arriving at the New York Hilton, the two large trunks containing my collection were wheeled into the lobby through the front door, and just as quickly wheeled out through the back door. The collection had been stolen in a matter of seconds by a man posing as a hotel porter. It was an utter disaster – the forty-five stolen dresses had taken months to design and make; they represented most of our samples for the forthcoming season – without them we would be lost.

In 1970, Richard Cawley became my assistant. He was a great character – flamboyant and very creative – and for twelve years he was my right-hand man.

Desperate to get the collection back, I offered a ransom – I went on television to make an appeal – and waited. By now the theft was big news and it was in all the newspapers, with dramatic headlines like, '40G Gowns Stolen & Designer Offers To Pay the Swiper', and 'Ransom offered in a Crime of Fashion'. My plight even featured in *The New Yorker* magazine and I received a telegram from the Mayor, Ed Koch, apologising on behalf of New York. Everywhere I went people recognised me; the story was on every newsstand and every TV channel. A little girl stopped me outside the department store, Saks Fifth Avenue, "You're the man who had his dresses stolen, aren't you," she said, "Well, please don't think we're all like that."

At first there was no response, then I had a 'phone call from the owner of a dress shop. It appeared that my precious dresses were being sold from the back of a truck in Harlem. The most bizarre part of the story came when I had a message from another 'lady', only this one was called Walter Jeff, and he was a 6ft tall transvestite drag queen who had acquired one of my dresses and worn it for a cabaret performance at a Harlem club the night before. He had rung NBC TV and announced he would be returning this dress to me at the Hilton and NBC were to be there to record the meeting. He arrived in drag, wearing his own dress and a big afro wig. My dress was in a sorry state, creased and sweat-stained, with a thick rim of stage make-up around the neckline. I wrote a cheque for the amount he said he had paid, but the story didn't end there. I understand he went straight to cash the cheque but the confused teller refused to process it – Walter Jeff was a man but the customer was dressed as a woman!

In New York the place to be was definitely Studio 54, which was about to celebrate its first anniversary with a big party. "Why don't you just ring up and say who you are," someone suggested, "Your story's everywhere, they're bound to let you in." So I rang and asked if my assistant, Richard and I could come and drown our sorrows. There was a pause at the other end of the 'phone, "Well we've been reading all about you – your names will be on the door." Once Richard and I were inside, it seemed we were definitely at the party of the year – the perfect place to take our minds off the loss of the collection. It was pure hedonistic spectacle, a fantastic celebration of uninhibited exhibitionism summed up by Rollerina, an exotic transvestite who roller-skated around the dance floor wearing a crinoline balldress and a tiara. Among the people we spotted were Truman Capote and Andy Warhol, Yves Saint Laurent and Bianca Jagger, Halston, and Issey Miyake. Liza Minnelli, dressed in a red Halston jersey jumpsuit, sang 'Happy Birthday'. I spoke to Karl Lagerfeld, whose hair was powdered white; he was charming and sympathetic, commiserating with me about the famous theft.

The Studio 54 party might have lifted our spirits but my nightmare was not over yet, and when I left New York without the collection the customs officials at the airport were horrendous. They demanded a duty payment of $30,000 because of the missing dresses. I showed them the telegram from Mayor Koch and a letter from the detective dealing with the case, but they maintained that if you brought clothes into the country you had to re-export them or pay the duty. I certainly didn't have the $30,000; they allowed me to travel back to London but I was to send a cheque the moment I got home. When I returned to England I wrote to the Mayor and pleaded with him to intervene. When he wrote back, he sympathised with my unfortunate experience, but explained that the law of New York must still be upheld. However, I never received a bill.

THIS PAGE, ABOVE The ransom handover: meeting Walter Jeff, April 1978 OPPOSITE PAGE Two coat designs from the 1970 Indian collection featured in *Women's Wear Daily* [October 1970 © The Condé Nast Publications Ltd] OVERLEAF LEFT Dramatic daisy print silk dress with matching ruffled cape [*Vogue*, July 1976. Photograph and © Barry Lategan] OVERLEAF RIGHT Striding out model Janice Dickinson in Bellville Sassoon's striking scarlet dress [*Vogue*, 15 March, 1979. Photograph Mike Reinhardt/*Vogue*. © The Condé Nast Publications Ltd]

LONDON —

THE LADIES LOVE THE
SENSUOUS INDIAN MOOD
OF SOME OF BELVILLE
SASSOON'S COSTUMES.

From the new collection
shown this month the best
seller is also one of the most
expensive. It's called "Jai-
pur." The brocade-bordered
dark green mole coat is closed
with heavy silk frogs. The
Midi coat goes over a dark
green wool dress in the same
length, also bordered with the
brocade (sketched right). The
London Ladies who ordered it
include Lady Rotherwick,
Lady Daphne Straight and
Mrs. Peter Cazlet. From the
U.S., Dru Heinz and Mrs. Pat
Munroe of Washington, D.C.

Belville-Sassoon also says a
"tall" member of the Royal
Family ordered it, but won't
reveal her name. It's known
that both Princess Margaret
and Princess Alexandra buy
from the house. Meg is not
tall.

"Rajputana" is another of
the popular Indian mood costumes. The pale cream wool
Midi coat is hand painted and
goes over a wool crepe dress
whose pleats are caught by
embroidered cross stitching
(left). Lady Beaumont of
Whitley, Lady Harlech. Mrs.
Charles Bishop and Fiona
Thyssen ordered this cos-
tume.

103

The Bellville Team, 1989

1980s

The '80s was another big decade for me, and for the company. In 1982 I took over the reins from Belinda after she formally retired from the company, although she remained a consultant for five years. We left Sloane Street and moved nearby to Pavilion Road, Knightsbridge. Life became more serious; the responsibility for running the company now lay solely with me, and I had to prove myself all over again. At this point, my sister Marguerite became a director and my brother Ronald became the company accountant. I felt very cosseted by my family – at a challenging time they came to help and support me, which meant a great deal. Their advice and guidance over the years have been invaluable, and not for the first time, I thanked my lucky stars I was not an only child!

As Belinda's retirement ended one Bellville Sassoon era, the arrival of Lady Diana Spencer as a customer heralded the onset of a new one. Our romantic style suited her, and the trousseau dresses we made for her helped bring about a resurgence in romantic balldresses. We were making so many clothes for Diana, it made us very newsworthy. The amount of publicity she generated was unprecedented. It also brought in a lot of American buyers who were always fascinated by Diana and what she was wearing. The royal wedding of 1981 struck an almost universal chord. Historically, royal weddings are seen as great unifiers, but this one in particular was to have a profound effect on the nation, and the bride would have an equally far-reaching influence on British fashion. The royal union symbolised a new mood of hope and renewal, especially after the severe economic difficulties and industrial unrest of the '70s.

When we moved to Pavilion Road one of our first visitors was Barbara Cartland, who would arrive by Rolls Royce wearing her signature Cartland pink. She came to see us several times but we tactfully advised her that we didn't have what she was looking for and she was better to stick with her Hartnell. Another eccentric visitor was Lady 'Bubbles' Rothermere, the great social hostess and wife of newspaper magnate, Lord Rothermere. She always left things to the last minute when she wanted something made. If she chose from the ready-to-wear, she would insist on choosing something at least one size too small – and there was no dissuading her. She had her own preferences for a dress: it was always rather too tight, rather too low, rather too full – and it all looked rather too much!

Belle Shenkman, a strikingly chic Canadian, was another of London's great hostesses and a great patron of the arts. Belle was certainly one of the best-dressed and most stylish women in London, and she became a special friend. She passionately loved clothes, and first introduced herself to me by announcing, "I'm used to being dressed by Balenciaga, and I don't expect anything less!" I first met Merrill Thomas, a socialite, in the early '80s when she was working as a freelance television fashion presenter. In 1982 I did a television series on TV-AM with Merrill called 'Style by Jury', in which we critiqued the wardrobes of famous celebrities, including those of Elizabeth Taylor, Bianca Jagger, and Margaret Thatcher. Merrill and I became very close friends and she acted as my muse. She would look at the collection and say, "Women of a certain age need a little help from their designer friends – you need more dresses with sleeves!" She is enormous fun and has introduced some wonderful clients like Shakira Caine. One day Faye Dunaway arrived with her husband, the photographer, Terry O'Neill, with her hair in rollers. I was to design a dress for her new film *Duet for One* (1986), based on the life of the cellist, Jacqueline du Pré. Faye was beautiful and charming and kissed me on the cheek when she left. However, there were problems on set

OPPOSITE PAGE Designer Lorcan Mullany joins Bellville Sassoon in 1987, adding a new dimension, and eventually his name to the label [Photograph Ben Coster] OVERLEAF LEFT Supermodel Yasmin Le Bon wears Bellville Sassoon's all-important cocktail dress in dusty pink duchess satin with ruched bodice, over-sized bow detail and short sarong skirt [Spring 1989. Photograph John Carter] OVERLEAF RIGHT Pink satin camellias decorate the strapless bodice of this draped bustle-back cocktail dress [October 1987. Photograph Natalie de Lamoral]

OPPOSITE PAGE The New Romantics: Bellville Sassoon's Dandy Buccaneer look, velvet doublet jacket with a froth of lace at the neck, feathered beret, and knickerbockers [Autumn 1981. Photograph Tony McGee] THIS PAGE Another trademark – party-style polka dots – with dog to match! [Spring 1987. Photograph Natalie de Lamoral] OVERLEAF Bellville Sassoon's individual take on bold prints continues into the Eighties. This Ascher print dress featured in the Victoria & Albert Museum's 1985 Ascher retrospective exhibition and is now in the V&A's collection.

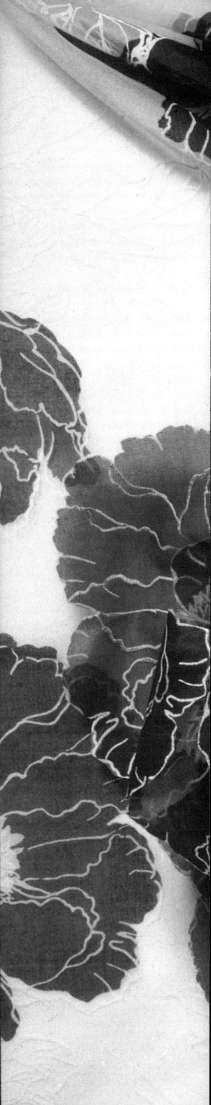

My assistant, Helen Storey

with the producer and Faye was replaced by Julie Andrews, who was very professional but rather cold compared to Faye – and not at all like cheery Mary Poppins!

In the late '80s, the fashion writer, Suzy Menkes invited me to a dinner party at her Primrose Hill home for the flamboyant French couturier, Christian Lacroix. Also invited were Zandra Rhodes, and Ossie Clark. Christian Lacroix arrived very late, straight from a fashion show he'd staged at the Serpentine Gallery. The highlight of the evening came when Suzy showed her collection of Ossie Clark dresses to Christian Lacroix, who was very complimentary. Ossie was so proud. The whole evening was delightful and it was a wonderful opportunity to meet Lacroix, who was really making a name for himself .

I have been very fortunate in having a succession of excellent assistants over the years. Richard Cawley left in 1982 when he won an Observer food competition and went on to become a successful cookery writer, often appearing on television, and now has numerous books to his credit. His successor was Helen Storey, a very talented girl. The daughter of the playwright, David Storey, she came to me in 1983, after working for Valentino and Lancetti in Rome. We got on extremely well – she understood what the requirements of our clientele were because she knew what couture was all about. I was very fond of her and she was with me for four years before she left to open her own business. When Helen left, George Sharp came to work with me as an assistant. He was an extremely gifted designer who drew beautifully. He had a great sense of humour and would draw marvellous fashion cartoons, some of which we used as our advertising. Over a period of fourteen years he became a director and a very important part of the company. I had a long and fruitful working relationship with him, which was of enormous importance in the creativity of our collections, particularly on the couture side.

In 1987 Lorcan Mullany joined forces with me as design partner. Although he had worked for Hardy Amies and Bill Gibb, he was an established designer in his own right, and his was a much more commercial background. He had spent virtually his entire career in ready-to-wear, but this was the way that the company was developing anyway. Couture was a smaller part of the company by then and Lorcan felt that expanding the ready-to-wear was the way to take the company forward. So George and I carried on with the couture clientele and Lorcan concentrated on the ready-to-wear – which all three of us worked on. It was a time of great excess, the decade of the yuppie and the supermodel. Fashion reflected this wealth with lavish entertaining, the rise of the logo-emblazoned accessory, and the influence of the cult soap-opera, *Dynasty*. For many women Dynasty-style shoulder pads became *de rigeur*, whether or not they were suitable or flattering. One customer came in and asked me to design a chiffon evening dress. It had to have a low neckline but, even more importantly, she said, the dress had to have large shoulder pads. I advised against this as we couldn't disguise them. Her husband informed me that his wife always had shoulder pads – they were even sewn into her nightdresses. He then explained, "She recently went into hospital and refused to go into the operating theatre until a pair of her shoulder pads had been pinned into the surgical gown."

There were two different aesthetics at work in the 1980s: a very structured look with exaggerated shoulders and short skirts, epitomised by the new power suit, and the soft romantic look pioneered by the young Princess of Wales.

ABOVE AND OPPOSITE PAGE Designs from the Autumn/Winter 1985 collection OVERLEAF LEFT Dressing up in silk tulle dress and stole, [December 1984. Photograph Bruce Weber/*Vogue*. © The Condé Nast Publications Ltd] OVERLEAF RIGHT Supermodel Cindy Crawford in lemon taffeta bow-bodice dress [*Vogue*, February 1987. Photograph David Bailey/*Vogue* © The Condé Nast Publications Ltd]

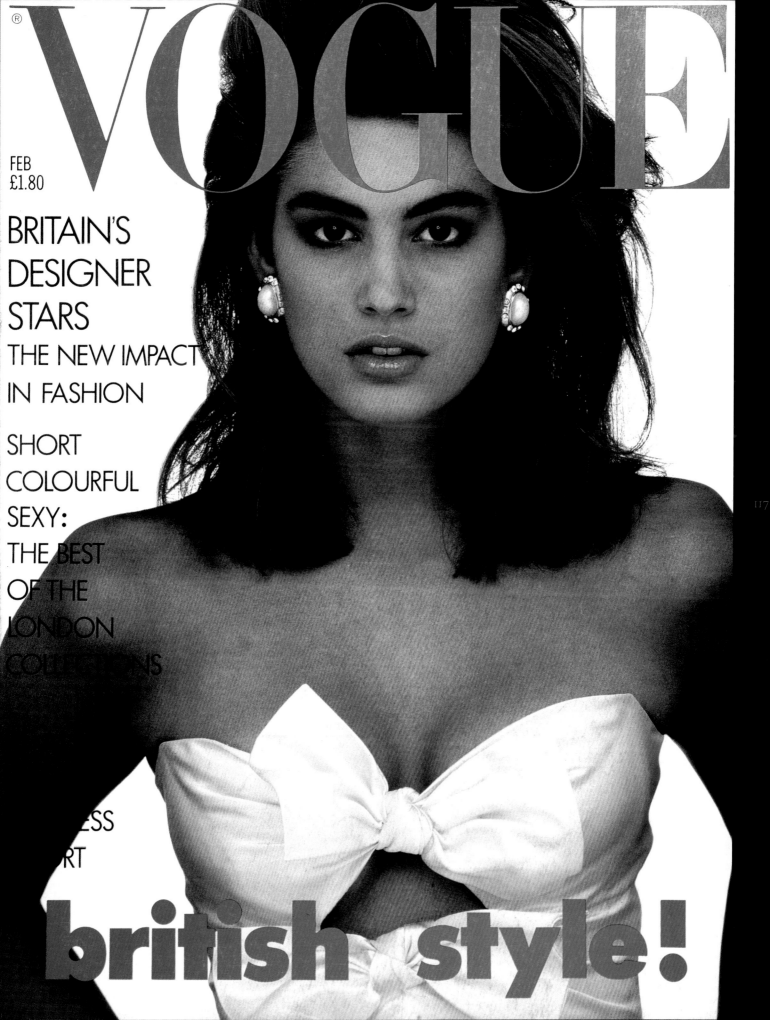

VOGUE

FEB
£1.80

BRITAIN'S
DESIGNER
STARS
THE NEW IMPACT
IN FASHION

SHORT
COLOURFUL
SEXY:
THE BEST
OF THE
LONDON
COLLECTIONS

ESS
RT

british style!

ABOVE AND OPPOSITE PAGE Eighties-style glamour: polka dots on white taffeta, extravagantly
ruched, swathed and gathered into oversize roses to accentuate shoulders and hips, 1985

Polka dots galore: figure-hugging strapless bodices flare from large-scale bows at the hip into THIS PAGE A flamenco skirt and OPPOSITE A ruffled overskirt, 1985

125

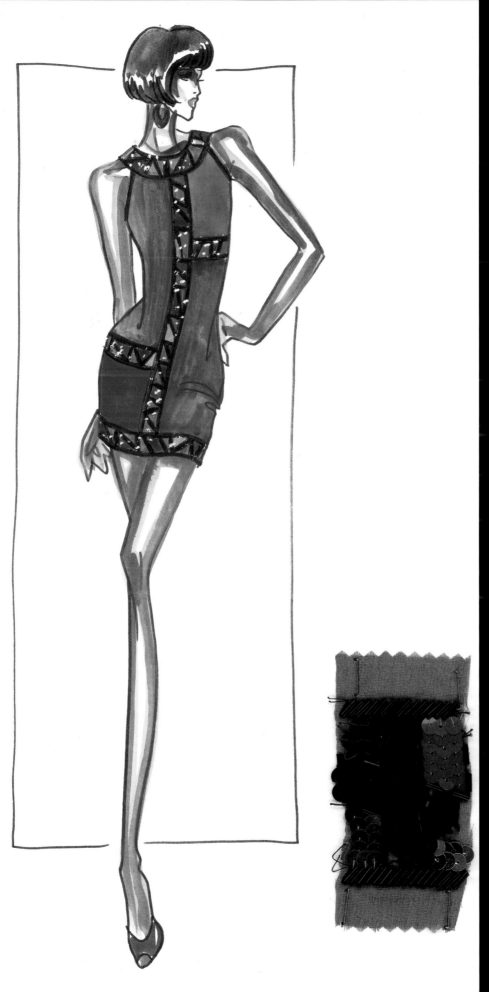

'The British are Coming: Part 2', Zandra Rhodes, David Bailey and me with Liz Tilberis in New York, 1998

Flying the flag: our Saks Fifth Avenue windows for 'The British are Coming: Part 2' promotion, 1998

1990s

In 1991 we moved to Culford Gardens, tucked discreetly behind the King's Road. There was a new mood of minimalism, and a season or two of Grunge, the dressed-down, messy, layered look that was the antithesis of everything we stood for. Luckily, it was short-lived, and although there were periods of economic gloom, you cannot suppress the urge women have to dress up and party.

The '90s established the cult of the corset as boned bodices and basques again became Bellville bestsellers. It was symptomatic of a return to shapely cuts and chic luxury, a follow-on from the statement dressing of the '80s, as women wanted to be glamorous and to show off their curves again. Worn with full skirts, often with layered net underskirts, this hour-glass look was a huge influence on evening wear as well as wedding dresses. Young, glamorous and modern, these bustier dresses were worn to everything from Oxbridge balls to the Metropolitan Museum's Fashion Institute galas in New York, as the romance of the '80s turned into the grand parties and new glamour of the '90s.

In the leaner '90s there was a new definition of glamour as the cult of the supermodel gathered pace. Among our designs featured in *Vogue* during the decade were images of Shalom Harlow dancing on a beach in a shell-pink satin column dress [May 1995], Linda Evangelista in a black velvet and satin bustier [November 1993], and a vivid green duchess satin trench coat [January 1996], Stephanie Seymour in a white crepe jersey goddess dress [June 1995], Trish Goff, demure in a silver satin shift [May 1996], Stella Tennant in a slinky black bias dress [December 1996], and Honor Fraser in a short dress of fuchsia satin and black guipure lace [December 1996]. 'Glamour is back', announced *Vogue* in its November 1993 issue, but this was an altogether more polished, grown-up glamour – less romantic fairy tale, more smooth sophisticate. As *Vogue* pointed out when describing one of our more minimalist dresses, 'devoid of detail, free from fuss, some of the most beautiful evening dresses need no adornment'.[19]

In September 1998, Saks Fifth Avenue sponsored a major British promotion in their New York store called the British Invasion, Part 2, inspired by Diana Vreeland's earlier famous exclamation in 1963. Saks dedicated its windows along Fifth Avenue to the Best of British designers and I was invited as one of the British designers along with Alexander McQueen, Julien Macdonald, Zandra Rhodes and Philip Treacy. Liz Tilberis, the then Editor-in-chief of American *Harper's Bazaar*, whom I knew well from her days in London when she was Editor-in-chief of British *Vogue*, co-hosted a dinner for all the visiting designers with Sting's wife, Trudi Styler. This was an Anglo-American affair; so that we all had the opportunity to meet each other, Liz arranged for each table to be hosted by an American designer, including Calvin Klein, Donna Karan, Mary McFadden, Isaac Mizrahi, Carolina Herrera and Bill Blass.

The high-octane gloss and glitz associated with the '80s developed into a revival of yesteryear-style glamour in the '90s, as couturiers scrambled to dress stars for the red-carpet events, which now received global press coverage on television, in newspapers and magazines. Our dresses were more in demand than ever and Bellville Sassoon Lorcan Mullany very much became a red-carpet label. It was the cult of celebrity married to the new opiate of the people – shopping – with rampant consumerism at all levels of the market from the high street to high-end luxury. As a result, individuality and discernible luxury became even more sought after to distance the client from high-street versions. It was altogether a more serious and sober time. As the decade drew to a close we learned, disbelievingly at first, of the sudden and tragic death of Diana, Princess of Wales.

LORCAN MULLANY FOR BELLVILLE SASSOON

ABOVE Nicky Haslam's design for the façade of Culford Gardens, 1991 OPPOSITE PAGE 'On the Town': fringed flapper minidress; in the background on the right, dressed up sailor-style, my assistant George Sharp, 1990 OVERLEAF LEFT Lorcan and I, portrait by Terry O'Neill, 1995 OVERLEAF RIGHT Graphic glamour in a black and white strapless satin dress [*Harpers & Queen*, March 1992. Photograph Stefano Massimo. © The National Magazine Company]

132

Apart from Dusty Springfield in the '60s, I've designed dresses for many concert artists, among them Barbra Streisand, Dame Shirley Bassey, and the opera star Kiri Te Kanawa, however, it is a famous musician of whom I'm most fond. Kyung Wha Chung, one of today's greatest violinists travels the world and comes to me for her concert dresses. I first met her when I made her wedding dress in the '70s and it turned out that she lived nearby. Later, when she had a young child it was difficult for her to practise so I offered her my house, which was empty during the day. After work, I would: often come home and sit on the stairs listening to her exquisite playing – it was quite magical. As a violinist, ease of movement is of paramount importance – she prefers strapless styles, without sleeves to impede her playing. She invites me to her London concerts so I see her performing in my dresses – I always send her flowers and she always takes her final bow holding my bouquet.

THIS PAGE LEFT Red crepe dress with lace-panel back, 1999 ABOVE With international concert star, violinist Kyung Wha Chung in Bellville Sassoon, Winter 1994 OPPOSITE PAGE Specially commissioned, a hand-embroidered, gold bead couture dress made for Madonna, 1999

Marc Factor
Promotion dress
for Madonna
March 1999.

OPPOSITE PAGE Asymmetric minimalism: hand-embroidered, flower sequin sheath dress, 1997 [Photograph Angus Ross] THIS PAGE Dramatic red taffeta strapless bustier dress with jewelled embroidery and voluminous overskirt for maximum impact, 1991

139

OPPOSITE PAGE Sumptuous ball dress with overskirt in aquamarine and gold brocade recalls the golden age of couture [*Harpers & Queen*, December 1990. Photograph William Garrett. © The National Magazine Company] THIS PAGE The original Bellville design

2000S

Now we are into the new century and the noughties. George left in 2002, and Romy Gelardin came to us as an assistant designer, having worked with Valentino for fourteen years. Lorcan particularly enjoyed working with Romy and respected her knowledge of red-carpet dressing. Romy had a woman's understanding of our clients' lifestyle; because she led a very social life herself, she knew well the type of client who would wear our dresses. She drew beautifully and managed to add great style to the collections, successfully bridging those two important fashion worlds: couture and ready-to-wear. After Romy left, I had a new assistant, David Boughton, who also has a wonderful feel for couture. Lorcan has had a huge impact on the company and for the past two decades we have been designing together. He has strongly influenced the mood of each collection, taking it in a more commercial, ready-to-wear direction. In this way he has helped to ensure that the label remains current. New blood in an established company is a vital force and an exciting way to develop the brand. We are very simpatico and our ideas blend together to make a strong and distinctive image.

What began fifty years ago with a tiny skeleton staff in "thimble-sized" premises has flourished and developed into one of London's most consistent and successful design companies and Britain's foremost evening wear brand. Unlike many of the fashion businesses that sprang up in the heady days of the '60s, Bellville Sassoon has shown it has commercial staying power as well as creative success. Throughout each of the decades the label has proved it can move with the times, reinventing and reinterpreting glamour for the contemporary international fashion stage. My partnership with Belinda lasted for twenty-five years; my partnership with Lorcan of twenty-odd years is almost as long. We now dress the new generation of stars, young actresses like Rosamund Pike and Anna Friel, and glamorous singing sensations, Leona Lewis and Katherine Jenkins. Another traditional thread from the '50s and '60s that continues today is that mothers still bring their daughters to us. And our clients have remained remarkably loyal: Madame Fattal first bought from me in 1959 and is still a dedicated customer. She also brought her two daughters to Bellville Sassoon for their wedding dresses. Sharon Osbourne, the effervescent music producer and international television star, loves our special brand of glamour; her daughter, actress and singer, Kelly Osbourne, has also chosen Bellville Sassoon for red carpet events, and recently remarked that wearing it, she felt like a lady for the first time. How fashion has changed and yet come full circle.

We specialise in a very British brand of grand chic – the sort of caterpiller to butterfly transformation that comes when a women really adorns herself. All women have the desire to look wonderful and we give them the dresses to do so – designs that catch the eye with brilliant colour, luxurious fabrics and intricate hand-beaded embroideries. You have to find your own niche; you cannot be all things to all markets. My philosophy of fashion is that I like to make the kind of clothes that flatter. If you make a woman feel good, she automatically looks good.

So, right from the swinging sixties and into the new century, Bellville Sassoon has kept its finger on the glamorous pulse of contemporary fashion as it explodes, excites and evolves, always looking forward to the future – which is now Bellville Sassoon Lorcan Mullany.

140

THIS PAGE, TOP Backstage after the show, with Lorcan, my assistant, David Boughton, and models [Spring/Summer 2004] MIDDLE Romy Gelardin and Lorcan fitting a model [2003] BOTTOM With Lucinda Chambers, *Vogue* Fashion Director, at the Fashion and Textile Museum [2004] OPPOSITE PAGE Aquamarine embroidered lace dress [June 2004. Photograph Jenny Hands]

THIS PAGE AND OPPOSITE A selection of evening
wear sketches, 2003-2004

FEATHERS

INNER
ZIP
PLEASE

Summer 2002

THIS PAGE Jerry Hall in red lattice crepe satin dress [June 2006. Photograph and © Clive Arrowsmith at Camera Press] OPPOSITE PAGE Oscar-winning actress Helen Mirren in ruched chiffon dress [*Women & Home*, January 2008. Photograph Trevor Leighton © IPC Media SouthBank]

LEFT Gunmetal hand-embroidered net evening dress [Winter 2007. Photograph Ch
Troman] OVERLEAF Black organza strapless dress with rose detail skirt, [Winter
Photograph Charlie Troman]

ROYALS

ROYALS I am probably the only designer around today who has dressed all the female members of the royal family, apart from the Queen and the Queen Mother. Starting in the '60s, my royal commissions span a period of more than forty years, and a host of memorable dresses for a roll call of special royal clients – from the starry glamour of the young Princess Margaret to the arrival of the photogenic and captivating Diana, Princess of Wales. During my fifty years in the fashion world I have seen many changes in the way in which women dress, but for me, none is more interesting than the change in royal style.

I have also witnessed a major change in the way designers are perceived. My first visit to fit a member of the royal family was memorable for the pomp and circumstance that characterised it. I remember distinctly that we had to enter via the tradesman's entrance! Twenty years later, though royal protocol and deference were still required, there was also a new informality. This time I found that the role of designer had been upgraded – I entered through the front entrance. How times have changed!

Internationally, each fashion centre has its own cachet, its own speciality. Paris might have the sophistication of *haute couture*, America, the glamour of Hollywood and its stars, but London has the ultimate: the prestige of Royalty. There is nothing to compare with the distinction of royalty; royal clients are simply like no others. As Suzy Menkes, doyenne fashion writer, reflected, "French designers may have mighty fashion empires trailing clouds of fragrance. The British bask in the glow of royal patronage."[20] Back in the '60s, London had two different schools of couture that catered for the royal family: the 'old school' style of designers like Norman Hartnell and Hardy Amies, following in the great British tradition of court dressmakers, and a younger style, which is what we at Bellville were all about.

Royal weddings, overseas tours, state occasions and receptions – all the constant official entertaining that the royals have to take part in – provide London couturiers with our most prestigious clientele. The kudos of royal patronage has its own trickle-down effect – the peeresses, duchesses, ambassadors' wives, the ladies-in-waiting…they all need those special dresses suitable for the grand royal or formal occasion. Add to this the power of the press coverage that such customers generate and you have a potent couture cocktail, and a very distinguished clientele.

Initially, Belinda considered the royals to be her personal domain, not surprising when the press hailed her as, 'Belinda Bellville, top people's darling… that talented royal couturière', while I was her 'brilliant young co-director, David Sassoon'.[21] She was especially fond of Princess Alexandra – they shared the same sense of humour, and would often disappear into a private fitting room for a good gossip. However, Belinda was a stickler for etiquette: staff who might come into contact with members of the royal family had to master walking backwards out of the fitting room, curtseying correctly, and the proper manner of address for each royal. She was very strict about it all – a couturier to the royals was expected to follow protocol, and, above all, to be discreet. We even had a separate entrance and a separate fitting room for the royals at our premises in Cadogan Lane.

We dressed many of the Queen's immediate family, including Princess Margaret, and Princess Alexandra. We also dressed several of the Queen's ladies-in-waiting, and several ambassadors'

BUCKINGHAM PALACE
29th JULY 1981

The card and monogrammed presentation box from Buckingham Palace, which contained a piece of royal wedding cake, sent after the July 1981 wedding of the Prince and Princess of Wales

With best wishes from
Their Royal Highnesses
The Prince & Princess of Wales

wives. We frequently dressed guests who had been invited to stay at Windsor Castle or Balmoral. Although the Queen was not a Bellville customer, she was often surrounded by our designs, and she certainly knew a Bellville when she saw one. On one occasion, three of our customers were invited to stay with the Queen at Windsor during Ascot week. For this visit we made a couture evening dress for one of the Queen's ladies-in-waiting to wear. When the guests came down to dinner on the first evening, three guests appeared in the same Bellville dress. These Bellville-clad ladies were from very different walks of life – apart from the lady-in-waiting, one was Mrs David Bruce, wife of the American ambassador, the other was the actress Sheila Sim, wife of the actor Richard Attenborough. Not everyone tells us where they plan to wear their dresses, and even when they do, last-minute changes of mind can't be ruled out – which is exactly what had happened here. The ladies were not amused – but the Queen was. As they were all presented in their evening finery, the Queen looked at each dress, and with a twinkle in her eye, said: "Bellville! Bellville! Bellville!"

It was sometimes quite a challenge to juggle dressing so many royal ladies at once. By the '80s we were dressing the Princess of Wales, Princess Alexandra, the Duchess of Kent, Princess Michael of Kent, Princess Alice of Gloucester, the Duchess of Gloucester and the Duchess of York. They all had their own preferences and they all needed different things, sometimes for the same occasions, and sometimes they wanted to wear the same dresses. All the royal ladies have their particular foibles – the late Princess Alice of Gloucester had just one test for a good dress – could she curtsey comfortably in it? At fittings she would solemnly perform her curtsey in front of a mirror to try out her choices. Princess Margaret remained wedded to her waspie corset endlessly in pursuit of her youthful hourglass figure. Princess Alexandra would never wear short skirts or low necklines, while the Duchess of Kent would insist on over-fitting her dresses, and we would be forever taking things in and then letting them out. A royal couturier's life is never easy, but I am immensely proud and grateful to have dressed so many wonderful royal ladies – and I've had great fun along the way.

PRINCESS ANNE Our first royal commission came in 1960, and it all started with a ten-year-old princess. We were invited to design a special bridesmaid's dress for Princess Anne. She was to be a bridesmaid at the wedding of Lord Mountbatten's daughter, Lady Pamela, to the interior designer, David Hicks, at Romsey Abbey. This was to be a very high-profile society wedding; most of the royal family were to attend, and it would be Princess Anne's first appearance as a bridesmaid.

I had never designed for children before, so this was a whole new experience for me. It was Belinda who went to the first two fittings. However, heavily pregnant at the time, she was not well enough to attend the final fitting, and so I went in her place, accompanied by Sydna Scott and our fitter, Sybil. I was both excited and apprehensive about going to Buckingham Palace. On arrival we were met by a liveried page, who escorted us up to the nursery floor. Walking along the wide corridor, we passed glass cases filled with antique dolls that had belonged to earlier generations of royal children. We were shown into the nursery, where I noticed a large ink stain on the carpet, and there we met first the nanny, and then Princess Anne, who had braces on her teeth, and wore sensible sandals with white ankle socks. The nanny immediately took charge of the fitting.

When Anne stood proudly in her first long dress, twelve-year-old Prince Charles appeared, in order to inspect his sister's outfit. He wore a grey flannel suit with short trousers and proceeded to walk around his sister with his hands clasped behind his back, just like a miniature version of his father. Then the Queen entered. I quickly stepped backwards to make a polite bow and put my foot straight into one of the corgis' water bowls. I stood frozen to the spot, with water all over my shoes as well as the carpet. The Queen pulled a cord by the side of the fireplace, and another liveried page appeared, wiped my shoes and the carpet, and left. This wasn't exactly what I had planned for my first visit to the Palace.

At the previous fitting with Belinda, the Queen expressed her approval of her daughter's new dress, but, ever practical, had just one question: "Will it wash?" The bridesmaid dress must have been a success because before long we were asked to design another dress for Princess Anne, who was now in demand as a bridesmaid. This time it was for the 1961 wedding of Katherine Worsley to the Duke of Kent. Princess Anne's dress and matching capelet were in white organdie trimmed with yellow silk rosebuds. Both these bridesmaid dresses received extensive press coverage and set us on the royal path.

I next met Princess Anne when she was eighteen. She appeared out of the blue at our shop with a lady-in-waiting. It was the late '60s, by this time Bellville Sassoon had branched out into ready-to-wear, and it was from this collection that Princess Anne chose a dress. When Belinda found out about the dress she felt it was too old for the Princess, and that she should have chosen something a little younger instead. Belinda rang the Palace to speak to the Queen's lady-in-

THIS PAGE Princess Anne makes her debut as a royal bridesmaid in Bellville et Cie in 1960. For the wedding of Pamela Mountbatten, daughter of Lord Mountbatten, to interior designer David Hicks, the Princess wore a shawl-collared crinoline style in ribbon organdie. OPPOSITE PAGE Forty years later, Princess Anne reminisces about the dress during her visit, in 2003, to celebrate Bellville Sassoon's 50th anniversary.

waiting and did her diplomatic best, only to be told, "The Queen thinks it's wonderful and just right." So we left it at that. However, that wasn't quite the end of the story as Cecil Beaton chose to include this dress in his 1971 exhibition, 'Fashion – an Anthology', at the Victoria and Albert Museum.

In 2003, I met Princess Anne in quite a different capacity. As President of the UK Fashion Export Council, she came to visit our company as we were celebrating our 50th anniversary. During her official visit I reminded her of our first meeting and showed her the original sketches of the two bridesmaid dresses we'd made for her, which she found nostalgically amusing. She toured our workrooms, talking to the staff, and while I was showing her the collection, the Princess stopped to admire an elaborate embroidered jacket inspired by a blue Wedgwood plate. "Oh," she exclaimed, "We've got a whole room decorated just like this at Windsor!" After she left we got a call from the car, asking to have the jacket sent to Buckingham Palace because Princess Anne liked it so much.

160

THIS PAGE Princess Anne's hand-embroidered 'Wedgwood' jacket and matching skirt OPPOSITE PAGE The Princess wears the Wedgwood jacket at the State Banquet for President Sarkozy of France, Windsor, 26 March 2008 [Photograph Tim Graham. © Getty Images]

PRINCESS ALEXANDRA The same year that we made Princess Anne's first bridesmaid dress, we also started to design for Princess Alexandra. Apart from the Princess of Wales, Princess Alexandra is the royal for whom I have made the most outfits. Whereas the Princess of Wales was the most experimental and modern royal, to me Princess Alexandra is the most regally elegant. She is tall and attractive, but her traditional royal conservatism does not always allow her to emphasise her best features. Nevertheless, her way of dressing is very much in the best royal tradition – she dresses for the job!

From an early age Princess Alexandra had been taught by her mother, Princess Marina, who was noted for her own elegant style, what the requirements of a royal wardrobe should be. As a consequence, Princess Alexandra has set ideas on how she wants to look and has never really changed her style, although she certainly found one that suits her. She likes clothes with a touch of dash, and has always had a great feel for fabrics, and loves rich textures and colours. On her overseas visits, the Princess was often given gifts of fabric by foreign dignitaries, and she would bring in these souvenirs from her royal tours – jewel-like saris or lengths of beautiful hand-woven silks – and ask us to design something for her. At other times she would arrive with a wonderful necklace to try on with a particular dress we were making for her and she would tell us the fascinating history of the pieces.

While Princess Alexandra loves colour, she has her own preferred palette for her official wardrobe and has a special fondness for soft pastels and pale neutrals. These suit her perfectly and seem to mirror some of her favourite jewels: aquamarines, turquoise and pearls. The Princess is also very good in lilac, purple and tones of deep blue, and she was delighted with the peplum suit in cobalt blue that I made for her son's wedding in 1988. Not every royal looks their best at formal occasions but Princess Alexandra seems to excel at them. She has mastered the art of dressing formally without appearing either stiff or stuffy. Her height is a definite advantage, but so is her innate elegance. She favours soft, romantic dresses and tiaras clearly suit her, though she often jokes that they play havoc with her hair.

The Princess has great natural charm and grace, as well as a sense of fun – and although she has a regal air, she likes to be quite informal, and was one of the first of our royal customers not to make a fuss about royal protocol. Early in the 1980s Princess Alexandra asked the staff not to curtsey when she came to the shop, "I prefer to be like everyone else," she told us. The Princess is always considerate and appreciative, and likes to personally thank everyone who has worked on one of her dresses. She is particularly fond of Joan Forsberg, who has been her *vendeuse* and fitter for over forty years, and they have a great rapport. All customers get very attached to their fitters – it is a special relationship based on mutual trust and respect – and our royal clientele are no exception. Princess Alexandra is very interested in people and remembers everything, even the little things. She knows I have a sweet tooth and every Christmas I receive a box of handmade chocolates. She is very popular with everyone who has fitted her or helped to make one of her many outfits – especially me!

During the forty years we have been making for Princess Alexandra, according to royal tradition, she has never followed fashion just for its own sake, but she has always been true to her concept of what a royal princess should be and wear. And I must say she does it remarkably well.

Princess Alexandra often favours white or ivory for formal occasions LEFT A column dress of embroidered lace flutes into a chiffon mermaid skirt, 1989
MIDDLE AND RIGHT The picture of regal charm, Princess Alexandra dazzles in a flowing evening dress of white silk with silver dots, accessorised with a
royal order and diamond tiara, 1989. Photograph Tim Graham. © Getty Images]

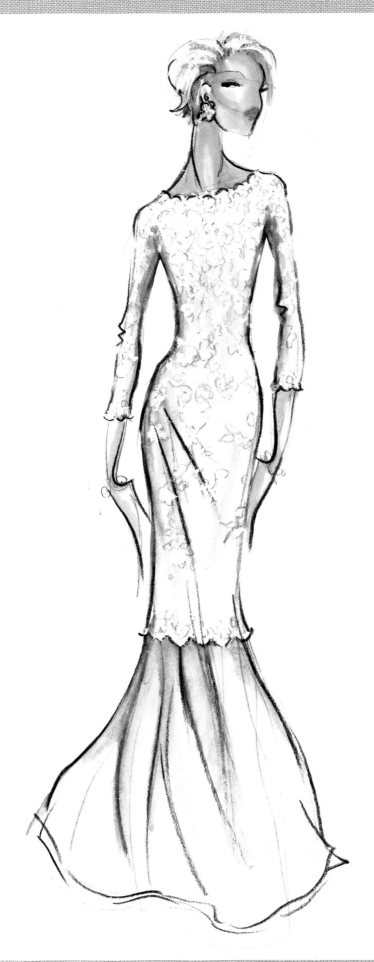

coat taff?
twrg
on aqua

THE DUCHESS OF KENT As a young woman, the Duchess of Kent was quite a trendsetter in royal style circles. She was introduced to us in the early sixties by her sister-in-law, Princess Alexandra. Katherine Worsley, as she had previously been, was newly married and looking for a couture wardrobe to suit her new royal role. The Duchess of Kent liked clothes. She was very into how she looked, and she always wanted to look outstanding, and until the Princess of Wales appeared on the scene she didn't have too much competition. Princess Alexandra, by contrast, didn't particularly want to be centre-stage; although viewed by the press as a stylish, young royal, she preferred a more low-key, understated presence.

The Duchess of Kent loved very strong bright colours and structured shapes – neat coats and little shift dresses, which suited her. She appreciated our emphasis on elegant simplicity, but she liked richly decorated styles too, especially our evening dresses. One of the younger members of the royal family, the Duchess of Kent's style was followed in the press, and copied. She was considered to be a well-dressed, chic royal, especially in the '60s when she really came to prominence. 'During her first royal assignment abroad,' commented *The Scotsman* in May 1963, 'the Duchess of Kent continues to delight with her combination of uncomplicated elegance and youthful awareness. Her choice of clothes shows a young love of colour and an adult appreciation of line. It is fascinating how this young woman, only a short time ago a typical open-air English rose, has developed into one of the smartest members of the royal family. Perhaps her choice of London's younger dressmakers has helped. Belinda Bellville is famous for her clean-cut youthfulness.'[28]

We did make an awful lot of couture for the Duchess of Kent, in fact at one point she was in so regularly that there was always something on the go for her in the workrooms. One trend that the Duchess launched on the fashion world was the caftan – the same "fashion pioneering" Bellville caftan that Vanessa Redgrave had been wearing. *The Daily Express* gave this fashion sighting headline treatment: 'Overnight, the whole exotic Oriental mood of fashion became respectable when the Duchess of Kent stepped out to the Royal Variety Show wearing her new blue organza caftan. Because, when royalty take to the caftan, it ceases to be a fancy dress and starts to be a serious fashion that many women will want to copy.'[29]

Unlike some of the other members of the royal family we dressed, the Duchess of Kent, like Princess Alexandra, always came to us at the salon for her appointments. Sometimes our royal clientele would flummox a young member of staff. Belinda kept a separate set of china, which was only to be used for our royal, or suitably VIP, clientele. One afternoon, during a fitting, I offered the Duchess tea and the junior brought down a tray with everything set out. When the Duchess attempted to pick up the cup she felt all round for the handle but couldn't find one – by mistake, the young girl, in a heightened state of nerves, had poured the tea into a sugar bowl, but luckily the Duchess saw the funny side.

We dressed the Duchess for many official royal occasions, including various Ascots and the wedding of Lady Diana Spencer to the Prince of Wales, but it was our evening dresses that were a particular favourite with her. She also introduced her attractive daughter to us, Lady Helen Windsor, for whom we made a number of formal things, including her outfit for the 1981 royal wedding. We continued to dress the Duchess of Kent into the '80s, and she retained her love of colour and a serene fashion confidence.

The Duchess of Kent was a keen follower of fashion and became a dedicated Bellville customer THIS PAGE wearing a silk coat, early 1960s [© Express Newspapers] OPPOSITE PAGE On tour in Uganda, the Duchess takes to the dance floor in a ruffled organza Couture dress, 1965 [© Express Newspapers]

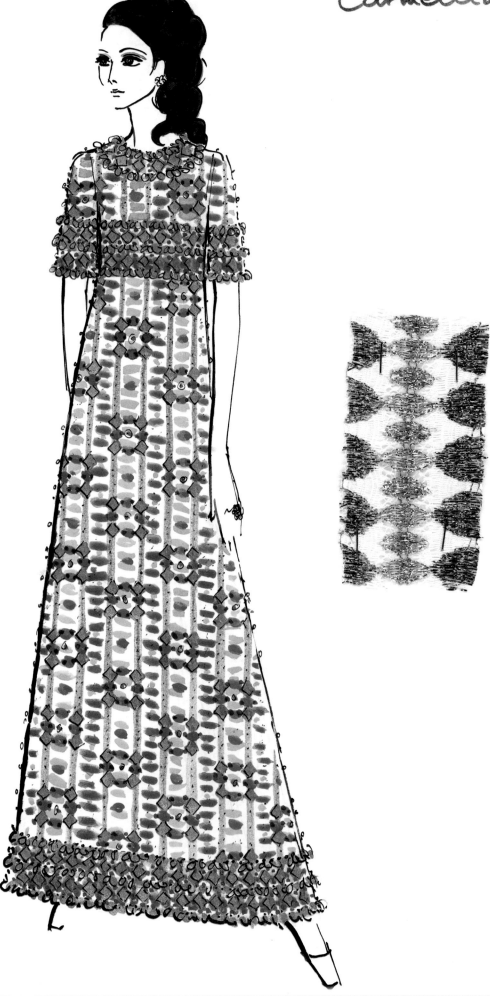

Carmelita.

OPPOSITE PAGE Sketch of a psychedelic sequin embroidered dress, 1967 THIS PAGE Royalty meets the stars, the Duchess of Kent in the same bold design face-to-face with Elizabeth Taylor and her husband, Richard Burton, at the premiere of *Doctor Faustus*, 1967. In her day the Duchess was considered by the press to be the young royal with a very current style of the '60s. For this occasion she chose our eye-catching dress which had recently been photographed by David Bailey for the cover of *Vogue* [© Associated Newspapers Ltd]

DUCHESS OF KENT CHOOSES ALMOND GREEN FOR YESTERDAY'S STATE OPENING

*D*IAMOND *necklaces, diamond tiaras, long white gloves and slim sheath dresses, mostly in pale greens and blues, was the glittering "uniform" worn by most of the peeresses at yesterday's State Opening of Parliament.*

The colours were obviously chosen so as not to clash with the scarlet robes of their husbands and the Queen's crimson velvet Parliamentary robe, which she wore over a slender white dress embroidered with gold.

One of the exceptions was Princess Marina, whose dress, worn with sparkling diamond tiara and necklace, was brilliant crimson.

Her daughter-in-law, the young Duchess of Kent, who was attending the State Opening for the first time, chose a more conventional colour. Her slim, springlike dress was of almond green, satin-backed organza. It is sketched here.

Belinda Bellville designed it with a youthful tie sash fastening the wrapover skirt, which reflected the Duchess's love of pared-down elegant simplicity.

The dress was lifted into the State Occasion class by being spangled on bodice and skirt border with delicate flowers embroidered in crystals and pearls.

Sketch by **BERYL HARTLAND**

Dressing the Duchess of Kent two decades apart THIS PAGE One of the first things we made for the Duchess after she got married was a dress for her first State Opening of Parliament in November 1962. *The Daily Telegraph* observed that the design in pale green silk embroidered in crystals and pearls 'reflected the Duchess's love of pared-down elegant simplicity.' OPPOSITE PAGE A more flamboyant style from 1988, pink wild silk with satin coin dots [Photograph Tim Graham. © Getty Images]

PRINCESS MARGARET In the '60s, at the same time that the Queen was being dressed by Norman Hartnell and Hardy Amies, we were dressing her glamorous younger sister, Princess Margaret. At that time Hartnell and Amies, founder members of the Incorporated Society of London Fashion Designers, were to our eyes the 'old guard' of British couturiers. Belinda and I consciously remained separate – we were the New Face of London couture. While the Queen stayed firmly with royal tradition, Princess Margaret, was more adventurous. By nature a party girl, she loved the razzmatazz of showbusiness.

Belinda always went for the fittings to the Princess's apartment at Kensington Palace, and sometimes there were surprises. On one memorable occasion, Belinda couldn't get anyone to answer the door, and tried the basement where she saw a light. The door opened a crack – and a voice asked "Who is it?" The door opened fully – it was Princess Margaret in a burgundy velvet Yves Saint Laurent suit over which she 'wore' a transparent polythene garment bag – she had made a hole at the top for her head and one at each side for her arms. To complete the outfit she was wearing rubber gloves and had a paintbrush in her hand – she was in the middle of whitewashing the conservatory walls. The Princess, quite unperturbed, apologised for the fact that no-one had answered the door, and invited Belinda to get on with the fitting. Despite Princess Margaret's reputation for being imperious and demanding, with Belinda and the fitters, she was always solicitous and charming. The Princess could also be engagingly down-to-earth, like her sister. Once, Joan, our fitter cut her finger and was very embarrassed when it bled, "Oh, ma'am, I'm so sorry about this," she apologised repeatedly. Princess Margaret seemed concerned only for Joan, "Oh, do let me put a bandage on it for you," she said, disappearing into her dressing room and returning with a plaster, which she insisted she put on Joan's bleeding finger herself. Princess Margaret's wardrobe was highly organised, down to the last detail, and nothing was left to chance. Kept in immaculate order behind a row of mirrored doors in her dressing room, each outfit was labelled with its own name. Lists on the inside of the wardrobe doors noted not only the name of each dress, but itemised the particular accessories to be worn with it – "white peep-toe shoes, white handbag, short white gloves". These were stored alongside, so that each outfit was totally prescribed and prepared. We were fascinated that everything was so strictly regimented. It seemed to us a particularly rigid system, but it wasn't until twenty years later, when Diana appeared on the scene, that experimentation and spontaneity really entered royal fashion.

Princess Margaret was a stunning young woman. Blessed with beautiful creamy skin and periwinkle-blue eyes, she was like a royal version of Elizabeth Taylor – she had a natural, sparkling glamour and adored the limelight. The fashionable '50s silhouette of nipped-in waist and full skirts of Dior's New Look was her favourite style and suited her curvy hourglass figure. For her American tour in 1965 Belinda and I designed some beautifully embroidered Empire-line dresses which were really fit for a princess. This was Princess Margaret's first official tour of America and she was accompanied by her dashing young husband, the Earl of Snowdon. The glamorous couple were fêted and photographed wherever they went, and the Princess's outfits were the subject of much scrutiny and discussion in the American press. *Women's Wear Daily*, rated her outfits from 1 to 5. Belinda and I were thrilled that our designs got 5-star ratings![54] During the visit, some of Princess Margaret's clothes provoked criticism as well as admiration. One paper referred to her fur coat as a 'moth-eaten mink'. The Princess was not worried – at home on her dressing room table, she had two separate 'For' and 'Against' correspondence trays. One for letters in praise of her clothes, the other for those that were critical. "Well, if they want to make me a gift of a new mink coat," she commented drily, "I'll be very pleased to accept it!"

OPPOSITE PAGE Princess Margaret was the first to introduce glamour to the royal family; in her youth she was the regal 'It Girl' of her day. Sophisticated and self-assured, during her US tour in 1965, she attracted acres of headlines and was surrounded by American paparazzi. Seen here leaving the Hollywood Palladium wearing Bellville Couture – a sapphire coat in Bernat Klein's ribbon tweed over a silk dress with ostrich feather hem, November 1965 [Photograph and © Reginald Davis, MBE]

Oleander.

A dress fit for the White House – one of the outfits we designed for Princess Margaret's tour of America in 1965. To our delight, the Princess chose to wear our pink gazar dress and jewelled jacket to meet the President THIS PAGE Original Bellville Couture sketch OPPOSITE PAGE *Life* magazine put Princess Margaret on its cover, dancing with President Johnson, November 1965 [Photograph Mark Kauffman © Getty Images]

LIFE

In Color
MEMORABLE NIGHT AT THE WHITE HOUSE

President Johnson
dances with
Princess Margaret
as Lord Snowdon
leads Mrs. Johnson
onto the floor

DECEMBER 3 · 1965 · 35¢

179

Two gala occasions OPPOSITE PAGE Princess Margaret enchanted the American press in a cream silk dress embroidered with gold and silver flowers when she met Hollywood's 'high society' at a star-studded banquet in Beverly Hills, November 1965 [© PA Photos/AP] THIS PAGE The Princess meets the Beatles and their manager, Brian Epstein, at the premiere of *Help!*, 29 August, 1965 [© PA Photos]

PRINCESS MICHAEL OF KENT We first met Princess Michael of Kent in 1978, through the recommendation of Beatrix Miller, the then editor of *Vogue*. Baroness Marie-Christine von Reibnitz, as she was then, had just got engaged to Prince Michael of Kent and she asked us to design her wedding dress. A statuesque and striking beauty with wonderful blonde hair, I found the Princess to be a delight-fully easy person to get along with. She had very definite ideas about how she would like to look on her special day. As it was for her second wedding, the design wasn't strictly speaking a traditional wedding dress. Instead, we created a romantic Edwardian style in cream crêpe de Chine with Chantilly lace inserts, which was designed for the church ceremony. Then, just two weeks before the wedding, the Baroness learned that she wouldn't be able to marry in church. There were complications: she was both a Roman Catholic and a divorcée and the Pope had decided to withhold the necessary dispensation, although the couple had previously been assured it would be granted.

Everything had to be entirely re-thought with very little time. Although a long dress was now out of the question for the civil ceremony in Vienna's town hall, Princess Michael of Kent, as she now was, wore our dress at the grand wedding ball held that evening at Vienna's Schwarzenburg Palace. With it she wore her husband's wedding gift to her, a beautiful diamond tiara that had been worn by both Princess Marina and Princess Alexandra at their weddings. I was extremely touched to receive a special telegram of thanks on the day of the wedding.

Back in London, Belinda and I were invited to a special reception at St James's Palace for all the friends and family who had not been able to attend the new royal marriage. Princess Michael looked radiantly happy and very glamorous. Among the guests I spotted were Mrs Jocelyn Stevens, Beatrix Miller, Lord Snowdon, and Norman Parkinson. Belinda and I knew how much the Princess loved her wedding dress, but, interestingly, her wedding day was not the only occasion on which the Princess wore it. She became the first royal bride to flout convention and wear her wedding dress at an evening party a few years later – something that was unprecedented for a member of the royal family.

In 2000, I asked Princess Michael if she would be a royal patron of Zandra Rhodes's Fashion and Textiles Museum, as I was one of the trustees. She was delighted to accept and was a great asset in her role as royal patron. The American Friends of the Museum who came to London were particularly in awe of the Princess, who was guest-of-honour at a special lunch at the Orangery in Holland Park. Whenever we asked for her help, Princess Michael was always very positive and very supportive, and this really impressed us.

For me, Princess Michael is the member of the royal family who is perhaps the most naturally stylish. She loves large sweeping picture hats and knows how to carry off a really glamorous, even dramatic, outfit. She doesn't have that English county look; she has a more European sense of chic. There is something of Cecil Beaton's *My Fair Lady* elegance about her, hence the style of our wedding dress.

NNNN
ZC3C CLH106 EOF802 AWK0753 20002
GBXX CO AUWX 032
WIEN/TLX 32/31 01 0955

LHS1006

BELLVILLE SASOON
PAVILION ROAD
LONDON/S.W.1.

TO DAVID SASOON AND ALL AT BELLVILLE SASOON

A THOUSAND THANKS FOR MAKING ME LOOK HOW I SHOULD ON MY

SPECIAL DAY
        PRINCESS MICHAEL OF KENT

COL LONDON/S.W.1.

ABOVE Princess Michael of Kent, patron of the Fashion and Textile Museum, hosts a lunch for the American Friends of the museum at the Orangery, in London's Holland's Park, 2005 OPPOSITE PAGE Princess Michael of Kent in her wedding dress [By kind permission HRH Princess Michael of Kent] OVERLEAF LEFT The royal bride dressed in another romantic Bellville Sassoon design, and Prince Michael of Kent, photographed for *Vogue* by Norman Parkinson, August 1978 [© The Norman Parkinson Archive] OVERLEAF RIGHT Design for the Royal Ceremonial Dress Collection's 'Court Couture' event at Kensington Palace, June 1992, launched with a fashion gala in the presence of Princess Michael of Kent

Bellville Sassoon design for 'Court Couture '92'.

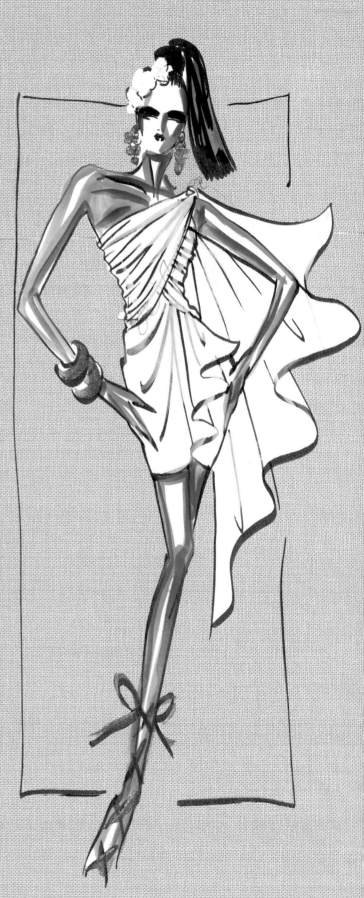

THE DUCHESS OF YORK Sarah, Duchess of York, was part of a new generation of royals, and came to me on the Princess of Wales's recommendation. Like Diana, Sarah was a recent addition to the royal family, an active mother, and quite informal, but that is where the similarities ended. Unlike Diana, her vivacity and strong will outweighed any sense of style. I first met her in 1987, when I received a telephone call from Ascot to say the Duchess was on her way back to London and would like to come to my shop. Her car arrived at 6.00pm with two motorcycle outriders and she made a dramatic entrance. "Mr Sassoon – may I call you David? – I'd love you to design some things for a foreign tour I have coming up." The Duchess had recently had a baby, and needed some formal dresses. So we took her measurements and she chose six outfits.

Thirty years after my first visit to Buckingham Palace to fit ten-year-old Princess Anne, there I was back again. Last time, I had to use the tradesman's entrance; this time we drove through the front gate. We were taken up to what had once been the nursery floor and was now a set of rooms for the Duke and Duchess of York. No sign of the liveried page who had wiped my shoes so long ago; instead, for the new generation of palace staff, a simple but smart uniform was the order of the day. We were shown up to the Duchess of York's bedroom, a mix of the formal and informal – lots of Colefax & Fowler-style chintz, and photographs of the Queen and Prince Philip and other members of the royal family. The bed was piled with masses of dolls and teddy bears, and there was the bunch of gold wedding balloons that had been attached to her going away coach. The Duchess bounced into the room fifteen minutes late, full of apologies. She'd put on 7lbs since the week before, which was upsetting her as she was trying hard to lose weight. We successfully fitted four outfits, and she asked us to make her some more. Whenever I visited the Duchess, my fitter and I would walk along the same grand corridor, with its wonderful views of the Mall, past magnificent portraits and fabulous pieces of furniture, and alongside all these was a tatty old wooden table that wouldn't have looked out of place in a garden shed. This table fascinated me, as it seemed so completely out of place, until one day the mystery was solved. I discovered it was used to cut and arrange the beautiful flowers.

Sarah, Duchess of York wasn't a great one for taking advice – she had her own ideas about how short and how fitted she wanted her clothes to be. But she did get better, and when she began to trust me, she also began to listen. I dressed her for five years and made clothes for several of her foreign tours to Canada, Australia and America. She was very bubbly, very charming, and always in a rush and late for her fittings. You couldn't help but be drawn to her natural exuberance. I remember one particular commission. Sarah asked me to design a white chiffon dress for a fancy dress party. It was to be Grecian in style – draped, with a plunging neckline, a bit naughty and nymph-like to show off her legs. To complete the outfit she had some beautiful white camellias flown over specially from America to wear in her hair. During the fitting, the Duchess went into the adjoining room to show the dress to Prince Andrew. "You can't possibly wear that," I heard him say, "It's FAR too short!" Sarah did not agree. "But you don't understand," she told him, "I'm supposed to be a Grecian goddess!" She did wear it – and she did look like a Grecian goddess!

DIANA, PRINCESS OF WALES It is impossible to overestimate the effect that Diana had on royal style, first as Lady Diana Spencer and then as Diana, Princess of Wales. Without a doubt, of all the female members of the royal family, Diana made the biggest transformation and the biggest impact. She sparked not only a national, but an international, cult and truly became an icon of the modern age.

Over a period of thirteen years, from 1981 to 1993, I made her more than seventy outfits. I dressed Diana for many of the most significant events in her life: her first official press photograph with the Queen, the engagement portrait for the Royal Mail's celebratory stamps, her first solo engagement, her going away outfit after the royal wedding, her first State Opening of Parliament, and the christening of Prince William, as well as for a host of official royal tours, state receptions, and those famous visits to charities.

I certainly got to know the Princess through the language of fashion, and it seemed at times that her choice of clothes directly mirrored the changes in her life. Initially a demure ingénue, Diana became a romantic fiancée, then a fairytale princess, a young hands-on mother, and an independent and charismatic woman.

When Belinda and I first met Diana, her face and figure were slightly chubby, but over the months of fittings, the weight fell away. She had beautiful skin and eyes, and lovely hair. She was slim yet still shapely, with long elegant legs. Before she came to us, like many girls of her age, Diana had casual clothes for her work as a kindergarten assistant, as well as good country clothes and some pretty evening things. Style-wise, she had a fairly basic Sloane Ranger wardrobe. What she didn't have were the formal outfits she now required for her new official role. It was at this point that Diana's mother, Frances Shand Kydd intervened and decided her daughter would have a designer trousseau. Immediately after the engagement was announced, she brought Diana in to see us. Frances Shand Kydd was already a customer of ours, and as is so often the case in the couture world, mothers introduce their daughters to their favourite couturiers – only this daughter was going to become the Princess of Wales.

As soon as the engagement was formalised, all eyes were on Diana. Before she came to us for her trousseau, Diana had rarely had anything specially made – it was a whole new experience for her. It wasn't a new thing for us – we knew all about the process and protocol of designing for a member of the royal family, yet this was something different. It was the challenge of designing for a young girl both before and after she became a royal. Diana was young and positive with a completely unstuffy attitude – she really was the most enchanting person. We were used to making dresses for similar looking upper-class girls with perfect skin and lovely figures, the modern versions of yesteryear's debs. Yet, Diana was different – she had absolute star quality. Her image, even her hairstyle, was totally different from any of the other royals. She had a youthful, almost coquettish chic, that made the world sit up and take notice. She took trends and made them her own. In doing so, she firmly shone the spotlight on British designers, and gave the British fashion industry an enormous boost.

The Lady Di look became the Princess Di look and girls and women followed suit in admiration, even adoration. It helped that Diana was on a fashion journey herself, finding her own style and identity. From being just another

187

Lady Diana Spencer chose a demure navy Bellville Sassoon sailor suit, LEFT AND OPPOSITE, for her first official photograph with the Queen and Prince Charles, after her forthcoming marriage was approved by the Privy Council in March 1981. [Photograph Fox Photos © Getty Images]

county girl from an aristocratic family, she was thrust into the royal limelight, and became the subject of an unprecedented media glare. Diana's style was quixotic, constantly changing and evolving. As her fashion confidence grew, she put her own stamp on contemporary chic. Among her early trademarks were frilled and ruffled collars and cuffs, pearl chokers, romantic balldresses, elegant flat shoes, and all became style must-haves.

Diana chose a demure navy-blue sailor suit from our ready-to-wear collection for her first official photograph with the Queen after the engagement was announced, which sparked off a trend for sailor collars. And there was a romantic ruffled blouse for the official engagement stamps, which set off another trend. When Diana first married Prince Charles she did conform to royal fashion protocol, but it didn't take her long to find her own style – at heart she was never a conventional royal.

The Princess of Wales reinterpreted and reinvigorated royal glamour and brought it firmly into the modern age, bringing with her a youthful approach, a love of colour and a flair for innovation and experimentation. She was as happy in jeans as she was in a balldress, and whether she was off-duty or appearing in a formal capacity, she always dressed with great style. For many royals, it was an effort to dress up; for Diana it seemed to come naturally. Contrary to popular belief, she didn't take fashion too seriously, but she enjoyed it, and always kept it fun. For Diana, fashion was fun, it wasn't a chore but a pleasure; she loved to dress up – she liked to star and surprise.

We had virtually no restrictions when designing for the Princess. For a start, she was extremely unusual – she had the sort of colouring that meant she could wear virtually any colour – and she did. Diana was the first to wear trousers and a tuxedo for a formal occasion, and she stopped wearing hats for many of her later engagements. It was typical of Diana's new and natural approach to meeting and greeting that she dispensed with gloves, until then a symbol of the divide between royalty and subject. Similarly, she was happy to mix costume jewellery, most often by Butler and Wilson, with her collection of family and royal jewels. She liked a sense of lightness in her clothes, reflecting her youthful *joie de vivre*. This was a new brand of royalty – and one that appealed, and seemed relevant, to people not usually interested in such things.

Diana came to us as a shy, young girl – interested in clothes, but with no real idea of what she wanted and needed for her new role. After this tentative beginning our relationship became friendly and much less formal, and I remember there was always lots of giggling and laughter during her visits to us. I noticed that Frances Shand Kydd left Diana to make her own decisions in the choice of dresses she would like to have. She was very diplomatic and never pushed Diana into anything she didn't want.

Diana always came on her own for her fittings before her marriage. She was very excited about the dresses – and loved seeing the finished effect. Her eyes would light up and she would twirl around in delight. By this point, interest in her had reached fever pitch, and the media followed her every move. The king of paparazzi, Richard Young, and the photographer and Tatler stylist, Michael Roberts, both tried to get into our showroom. They wanted to see our appointments diary to find out when Diana would be coming in. From then on we developed a form of code for royal appointments and Diana became 'Miss Buckingham' (while the Duchess of Kent was 'Miss Penny-wise').

Belinda and I were asked to design the going away outfit. Diana was quite definite about what she wanted to wear, and she herself chose the dress and bolero-style jacket as well as the colour,

Diana, Princess of Wales in the public eye THIS PAGE Wearing a Bellville Sassoon ruffle collar blouse for the Royal Mail stamps celebrating the royal marriage OPPOSITE PAGE At her first appearance at the Cenotaph Remembrance ceremony in November 1981, a Bellville Sassoon outfit reinforces her early fashion trademarks: large collars with pie-crust frills, bows, and strings of pearls

ABOVE AND OPPOSITE PAGE Just married: the going away outfit, July 29, 1981. The cantaloupe silk and the bolero jacket were chosen by the Princess. She loved large, romantic-style collars with frills and bows and wanted a straight skirt for the matching dress, which she felt was very sophisticated. We made two jackets, one with long sleeves, because she was worried about the weather. The Princess liked the suit so much she later wore it on several occasions, including her tour of Australia in 1983 [Photograph © Rex Features]

which we called cantaloupe. Diana was also adamant that the dress had to have a straight skirt, as she felt this was very grown-up, and the outfit was purposely trimmed with her trademark romantic ruffles. To cover all eventualities, there were two versions of the jacket: one with long sleeves in case the weather wasn't good, and the original version with short sleeves, which the Princess wore on the day.

Diana chose a jaunty tricorne hat from milliner John Boyd to wear with her going away outfit and one day she came to us straight from her final hat fitting, with a take-away coffee and she couldn't stop laughing. "I went in to get my cup of coffee," she explained, "and the girl behind the counter said to me, 'You look just like Princess Diana'." The Princess had instinctively replied, "That's the nicest thing anyone's ever said to me!" and the girl had been thrilled. Diana had kept her secret to herself, and she'd been giggling about it all the way to our fitting.

As the wedding day drew nearer, Diana lost a lot of weight and became very stressed – the strain of dealing with the media intensity was beginning to show. Perhaps too, it was the realisation of the enormous step she was about to take. At the final fitting she was very tearful and I sat her down and tried to comfort her. She had just come from the wedding rehearsal at St Paul's Cathedral and it was all getting too much for her. She told me she was worried because she hadn't thought about a handbag to go with our outfit, and now felt she should have one. So I offered to get one made in the same cantaloupe silk fabric. She was so relieved, she gave me a hug. When the bag was ready I put a handwritten card in the mirror compartment which simply said: 'Much happiness in your marriage and lots of luck on your great day'. The Princess later told me that she had found the note when she went to comb her hair before boarding the honeymoon train, and had been very touched by my good wishes.

Belinda and I were invited to the wedding, which was an incredible occasion and we felt immensely proud. Apart from designing Diana's going away outfit, we dressed her mother, Mrs Frances Shand Kydd, Princess Alexandra, the Duchess of Kent and her daughter, Lady Helen Windsor, and many of the other illustrious members of the wedding congregation at St Paul's Cathedral were wearing Bellville Sassoon. We had also made evening dresses for many of the same guests, including Frances Shand Kydd, for the pre-wedding ball at St James's Palace, which had been hosted by the Queen the previous evening.

There was a definite change in Diana after the marriage. At our first meeting, she had insisted we dispense with formalities; she called me David, and I called her Diana. Now we couldn't call her "Diana" – she was officially the Princess of Wales, so it had to be "Your Royal Highness". Previously, Diana had always come to us; now we went to her at Kensington Palace. However, Diana didn't go in for the normal formalities of royal protocol and at fittings, after the initial, "Good morning, your Royal Highness", the appointment would progress in a very informal atmosphere. She managed to strike a balance. The Princess could be charming and chatty, but nevertheless expected to be treated with the appropriate respect due her royal station.

After she was married, either the Princess or her lady-in-waiting, Anne Beckwith-Smith, would ring up with a brief regarding an event and ask for sketches. We would send a batch round and they would come back to us with Diana's pencilled comments, usually, "Yes, please!". The Princess of Wales was the ideal couture customer. She never

This is one
pease

fiddled with a fitting; she left you to do what you thought was right, unlike a lot of women who have dresses made for them and then want to over-fit and change everything. It was always a pleasure to make things for Diana. She wasn't grand — she was just very natural and easy to work with. In time, she became confident about her style, but right from the beginning, she was always very enthusiastic, and would instinctively say, "Oh, I love this!" as she tried things on. Diana had such style — she would really carry anything off. She was always polite and appreciative, and often sent thank you notes to let us know when a dress or outfit had been particularly successful. Later on, she would sometimes anticipate the effect of a dress, saying, "They'll love this", meaning the public and the press.

It was the evening dresses that we made for Diana that really hit the headlines. There was the red glitter chiffon dress that she wore for her first solo engagement, the premiere of the latest James Bond film, 'For Your Eyes Only' in June, 1981. Then the dress we designed for her first State Opening of Parliament on 4 November, 1981. Usually on this formal occasion, all eyes were focused on the Queen in her magnificent crown, splendid court dress, robe and glittering diamonds. However, this time it was the Princess of Wales in her Bellville Sassoon dress who drew everyone's gaze. But the dress that really captured the public's imagination was the one she wore to the 'Splendours of the Gonzagas' exhibition at the Victoria and Albert Museum the same evening. The exhibition displayed the treasures of the nobles of Mantua, but it was Diana who stole the show — for the second time that day! The dress was soft, pretty, and romantic, with an off-the-shoulder neckline and a full, floaty skirt — it was our contemporary version of a Winterhalter dress, in which the Princess looked like the embodiment of a modern fairy tale.

The Princess looked utterly charming and captivated the press as well as the public. We had a tremendous response, particularly from children who sent us drawings of Diana, telling us this was their idea of a fairytale princess. As one social commentator observed about Diana: "a very nice ordinary girl…had become a Cinderella princess."[25]

The next day when the Princess was at the Guildhall wearing one of our outfits again, the Palace issued a statement: the Princess was expecting her first child. Diana relied on us for most of her maternity clothes for both her pregnancies; some of these were still romantic evening dresses, others were colourful daywear. Dressing a royal mother-to-be was not really my strong point, but I think I got better at it the second time around!

In July 1982 I went to Kensington Palace to fit the pink crêpe-de-Chine print dress that Diana would wear for Prince William's christening. I arrived with the fitter and we were taken upstairs to the Princess's sitting room. The hall and stairs were carpeted in apple green with the Prince of Wales's feathers woven in cream, and the walls were pale peach with the plasterwork picked out in white. We fitted the Princess in her sitting room, which was decorated in turquoise. It was a friendly, personal room with an unframed photograph of the Prince of Wales carrying his baby son. Diana looked very well, she had already got her waist back, and was charming and full of high spirits because of the baby. But there was also a more sombre mood. Apart from the dress for the christening, we fitted a black dress for the Princess to wear at a memorial service for the Falklands War. It was also a

June 1981

ABOVE AND OPPOSITE PAGE Lady Diana Spencer in one of her early Bellville Sassoon trousseau dresses, in red glitter chiffon, meeting ballet star Rudolf Nureyev. She originally wore this dress for the premiere of the 1981 James Bond film *For Your Eyes Only* [Photograph Tim Graham. © Getty Images]

nov 1981

ABOVE Design for the State Opening of Parliament. It was the one time that Diana gave me specific instructions, see overleaf; the Princess later admitted it was a mistake to try to do my job for me! OPPOSITE PAGE At her first State Opening of Parliament all eyes were focused on the Princess, November 1981 [Photograph Fox Photos © Getty Images]

September 15th
1981.

Dear David,

Thank you very much for sending the sketches up – I have drawn in a rough diagram which I hope you can understand!

I wondered if it would be possible if the front & back could be of thicker material, almost as though it was padded!

If it's too difficult, for heavens sake let me know & if you could send up a sketch to what you think I mean, I'd be most grateful.

Again many thanks for taking the trouble,

Yours sincerely,

Diana.

September 17th
1981.

Dear David,

How terribly clever
of you to draw the exact
thing I wanted!

Could the back be the same
pattern as the front?

Many thanks for redoing
the sketch its going to look
lovely I'm sure.

Everyone up here went wild
about the lovely white dress!

Yours very sincerely, Diana

1981

ABOVE AND OPPOSITE PAGE The Princess of Wales in the white dress that was much admired at Balmoral, where guests 'went wild about it', as she explained in her letter of September 17, 1981. Originally worn at a Caledonian ball, the Princess is seen here wearing the dress at a State Banquet at Hampton Court for Queen Beatrix and Prince Claus of the Netherlands at Hampton Court Palace, November 1982. The Princess wears the sash of the House of Orange presented to her by Queen Beatrix. The dress is now part of the memorial collection at the Princess's ancestral home, Althorp

1981

ABOVE AND OPPOSITE PAGE Diana, Princess of Wales at her most romantic in a hand-painted, off-the-shoulder chiffon dress, at the 'Treasures of The Gonzagas' exhibition, at the Victoria & Albert Museum, November 1981. The young Princess loved this dress, which was part of her trousseau. It appealed to her sense of romance, and also reflected the romantic mood of early '80s fashion. A big skirt meant dressing up and she loved the idea of dressing up; she also liked the soft colours and the sparkle and glitter. It didn't disappoint her public – when she got out of the car with all the crowds and photographers waiting – there was a collective "aah!" [Photograph Tim Graham. © Getty Images]

204

THIS PAGE Diana, Princess of Wales in one of the Bellville Sassoon maternity coats she wore throughout her first pregnancy. She was wearing another of our maternity coats at London's Guildhall in November 1981 when the Palace announced she was expecting her first baby OPPOSITE PAGE The day after she wore a Bellville Sassoon coat with astrakhan collar and matching hat and muff for her visit to Gloucester Cathedral in 1982, the Princess was featured in all the newspapers, which hailed her chic new look. Harrods reported an unprecedented demand for similar coats, hats and muffs and the Russian look became mainstream overnight [Photograph Tim Graham. © Getty Images]

This one please

March 1982

ABOVE The royal seal of approval: the Princess wrote 'This one please' on the sketch of the white shimmer silk maternity dress she wore to the Royal Academy in 1982 OPPOSITE PAGE The Princess of Wales, pregnant with her first child, Prince William, wears the dress to meet Elizabeth Taylor, who was appearing in the play *The Little Foxes*, in March 1982 [Photograph © Express Newspapers]

Yes please!

March 4th 1982

ABOVE Diana so liked this striking and romantic 'Restoration'-style red taffeta maternity evening dress that she wrote 'Yes please!' on the sketch OPPOSITE PAGE The Princess wears the dress to the Barbican Centre, in March 1982 [Photograph Tim Graham. © Getty Images]

No roller like this ordinary stand no bow

this is dark blue pease

Feb. 1982

1982

Three maternity designs with Diana's comments written in pencil on each one. The blue velvet dress on the left has a deep collar and cuffs trimmed with antique lace that came from Windsor Castle and originally belonged to Queen Victoria

Bright pink
one
please

Please would I
have this one
what are
light colour
bow — colour
we are other
purple ...

distressing day as two IRA bombs had exploded in London – one at the Knightsbridge barracks and the other in Regent's Park. The Princess said she had heard the Hyde Park bomb go off and was clearly very upset by it. Ironically, when we arrived for the fitting, the palace security seemed very lax and no-one seemed to check who we were.

My visits to Kensington Palace were fairly frequent but on one occasion, I almost changed the course of history! I arrived at the Princess's apartment with my fitter, Nives, and we were ushered upstairs by the Princess's maid. I knocked on the door of her sitting room and then threw the door open wide for Nives, who was following behind me with an armful of dresses we were about to fit. To my horror, I knocked over three-year old Prince William who was standing behind the door. All I could think was, 'Oh, my god, I've killed the future King of England!' Diana rushed forward to cuddle and soothe her weeping son, and assured me all was well – the only damage was a small bump on the royal forehead.

Even when there was something the Princess did not like to wear, she presented a practical way round it, and triumphed. Diana once told me that apart from her maternity coats, she didn't usually like wearing coats at all. Instead, she was a great one for wearing thermal underwear. Even if it was going to be cold, she would say "Don't worry, David, I'll wear my thermals with this." There were exceptions: it was a particularly cold winter in 1982, and she wore one of our Russian-inspired coats, accessorised with our hat and muff, for a visit to Gloucester Cathedral. This outfit set off a *Dr Zhivago* trend. When she saw the astrakhan collar of the coat she said she would love a hat in the same fabric – and then a muff to match. It was the full Russian look, with the decorative looped frogging fastening on the coat, the astrakhan trims and accessories; that's what she wanted, that complete *Dr Zhivago* feel – romantic and dashing at the same time. In March 1982 Marylou Luther of the *Los Angeles Times* summed up the Princess's continuing impact: 'Last year she single-handedly brought back the ballgown. This year she seems to have inspired the Russian Cossack/ Dr Zhivago theme with her famous visit to Gloucester Cathedral. Princess Diana is credited with everything from restoring the monarchy to glorifying motherhood to initiating a kind of national dress-up campaign.'[26]

Although, the majority of clothes we made for the Princess of Wales were for formal occasions, I also made things for her private wardrobe. The Princess managed to develop and retain her own style despite the demands of her royal status. There was a clear distinction between her public and private lives and her clothes for these separate lifestyles; she came to us for both these different roles. She was the only member of the royal family whom I dressed in this way, both on and off-duty. Unlike some of the royals, Diana was easy-going and happy to have clothes from our ready-to-wear collections as well as the couture, and she could be quite spontaneous with her outfits, and her visits to us. She would say, "I need a dress for a party tomorrow night – can you make me something?" Or she would look through the rails and say, "What a lovely dress!" and buy it simply for the joy of it. She did not like endless fittings – usually just one or two were sufficient. On one occasion, Diana came in and wanted an all-white dress.

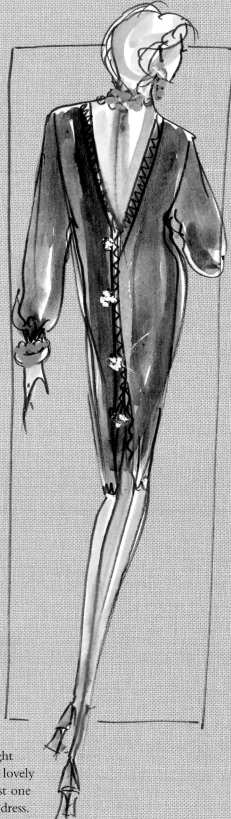

Diana had two very different types of wardrobe: a formal functions wardrobe and then a private wardrobe, and some of the things we made for her privately were never photographed by the press OPPOSITE PAGE Sketch of black wool jersey sweater dress with deep 'V' back and jewelled buttons, 1984 THIS PAGE Pink blouson jacket and long skirt, 1984

I picked one out. She put it on and was delighted – it fitted perfectly and didn't need altering. It was her favourite type of clothes shopping – in a very short time she had picked a dress and had it despatched to her. She later wrote me a charming letter to tell me it had been for a ball at Balmoral and had been a great hit.

The Princess often made surprise visits to the shop and one afternoon in August 1982 she arrived with Lady Sarah Armstrong-Jones, who had been a bridesmaid at her wedding. They had come to choose a balldress for Lady Sarah to wear at Balmoral Castle. It was to be her first long dress and Diana was going to help her choose, as she wanted it to be special. They had the shop to themselves, since it was officially closed for the August holidays, so it was quiet and private. Diana helped Lady Sarah try on all the long dresses and there was much giggling from the dressing room. In the end Lady Sarah settled on a scarlet taffeta strapless dress and they both left together like excited schoolgirls. Lady Sarah obviously adored Diana and listened to all her fashion advice. What struck me was the lovely gesture, typical of the Princess of Wales – she bought the dress as a gift for her young friend.

There was no mistaking it – Diana had star quality, but she also had a warmth and humanity that she was not afraid to show. She had an exceptional gift – the common touch – but there was nothing common about it. She had something special and unique, something that connected with and comforted people, especially those in less fortunate circumstances, whom she consciously reached out to, and in a modest way she used clothes to help her to do this. She was particularly conscious about her choice of outfit when she visited hospitals, children's homes, or hospices; when she was meeting children or the elderly. She liked to wear bright, pretty colours that would appeal to and hopefully cheer up those she was visiting.

The Princess of Wales had a great sense of colour. She understood that photographers like colour and she liked to surprise in fashion terms. If it was something that was going to catch the press or the public's eye, she enjoyed that. Although cutting edge fashion is not seen as appropriate for royal wardrobes – it is not how the public wish to see their royalty dressed – Diana wanted to please herself and her audience, those she was meeting, greeting and visiting and the waiting crowds who would also see her.

One of her most daring and original outfits was a richly coloured 'dressing gown' robe, worn for a grand government reception at Lancaster House in March 1985 to celebrate London Fashion Week. The look was very 'in' at the time, a fluid female version of the traditional smoking jacket; the Princess knew that this would be a high-profile fashion event and wanted to make an impact. She had ordered it from me some time before and I was wondering when she would be wearing it. It was flattering that she chose it for such a prestigious fashion event – but I was a little disappointed that she didn't go the whole hog and wear the matching trousers that originally made up the outfit.

Diana also found she could put her clothes to good practical use. After her divorce, her charity work became a more significant part of her life. At the suggestion of her son, Prince William, in 1997 she decided to sell some of her high-profile wardrobe at Christie's in New York to raise funds for two of her British charities, the Aids Crisis

Trust and the Royal Marsden Hospital Cancer Research Fund, and two American charities. The Princess handpicked 79 of her dresses and helped to write the auction catalogue notes on each one. This was an unprecedented sale, with a great deal of glamour, prestige and razzmatazz – and the international media loved it. The auction was a huge success and raised $3,259,000.

Two of our outfits were included in this special auction. One was a two-piece black sequin embroidered jacket and velvet skirt, which was bought by the French magazine, *Paris Match*, for $44,700. It was later featured in the magazine as a special competition prize. The other was a long black crepe evening dress with jewelled straps, which raised $23,000 and was bought by a delightful couple from California, who later came to meet me when they were in London.

I remember another incident to do with the Princess's clothes in 1996. I had a lunch date with Robina Ziff at the famous San Lorenzo restaurant in Knightsbridge, which was a favourite of Diana's. Robina, who had two London shops selling luxury designer womenswear, was running late and as I waited for her I saw that the Princess was sitting at the next table; she was also waiting for her guest and I wondered who could possibly be keeping her waiting. Diana tapped me on the shoulder and we chatted away until her brother arrived full of apologies. I noticed the Princess was wearing a very distinctive chain-print silk blouse. When Robina arrived she was about to remove her jacket when I realised she was wearing the same blouse as the Princess. So I whispered to her to leave her jacket on even though it was a very hot afternoon and Robina whispered back to me that she had sold the blouse to the Princess. Joan Collins arrived making quite sure everyone saw her but the lunch guests only had eyes for Diana. When the Princess and her brother left, Robina removed her jacket. At this, the group of Americans lunching at the opposite table, realising her tactful gesture, broke into spontaneous applause.

Diana's choice of clothes was at first romantic, and then grew more sophisticated, and increasingly independent, especially after her divorce from Prince Charles. The divorce marked a major shift in her wardrobe. Released from her marriage and her official royal role, and title, Diana could wear whatever she liked and no longer had to wear British designers. Her freedom – almost a rebellion – found expression in her choice of big brand European designer labels: Versace, Dior, and Chanel. During her engagement and marriage, Diana was conscious of her own height compared to her husband's, and tended to wear lower heels, even with her wedding dress and many of her evening dresses. After the divorce, there was a symbolic change: her hemlines got shorter, her heels got higher, and her dresses were noticeably sexier and more body-conscious.

There was a tremendous change from the shy young girl whom we initially dressed to this overtly glamorous woman. In her evolution from Sloane Ranger to style icon she transformed the royal image and royal style, paving the way for a new informality and experimentation among the younger royals – because of

OPPOSITE PAGE The multi-coloured 'patchwork' jaquard silk robe with quilted collar and cuffs and tasselled belt that the Princess wore to greet several hundred members of the fashion world when she attended a reception at Lancaster House to celebrate London Fashion Week, March 1985 THIS PAGE A curvy bouclé coatdress with contrast stripe revers, cuffs and buttons, which the Princess wore to church on Christmas Day, 1989

her, they were able to adopt a style that was less conventional, more sophisticated and fashion-forward. Throughout it all, Diana had an independent fashion spirit. Despite her royal status as the future Queen of England, she broke the rules of royal dressing – but the results were captivating and spectacularly popular. In doing so, she always strove to express and maintain her own individuality. It was refreshing to see someone so young and attractive not subsumed into old-school tradition. She brought a breath of fresh air to the house of Windsor. Diana made regal style contemporary – no mean feat, and Belinda, Lorcan and I are proud to have played a part in this.

Of course, it is not simply the clothes that I remember. Diana was very charismatic as a person, not just because she was a princess. There was something about her, you really did feel that she was special. She also had a certain vulnerability – you felt you would do anything for her. She had compassion because she suffered, too. She was a woman who shared her heart; she was human. I could see that she was a fantastic mother to her children, and that they always came first.

The last time I saw Diana was at the London preview of the Christie's auction. She looked wonderful – relaxed, suntanned, glamorous. I asked her what had happened to the going-away outfit, and if she planned to sell it. "No, I've still got it." she replied, "I want to keep that."

I feel blessed and privileged to have been part of Diana's story. Tragically, when I attended her wedding, I never dreamt that I would also attend her funeral. There's no doubting it, Diana left a lasting legacy – and how we do still miss her.

Daily Mail, Tuesday, July 21, 1992

HAVEN'T WE SEEN THAT FROCK SOMEWHERE BEFORE, YOUR HIGHNESS?

PAGE 13

Watching polo at Windsor

On tour in Lagos

Meeting AIDS patients in Sao Paulo

At Expo '92 in Seville

At the London Lighthouse

Very endearing, very enduring

LOOKS familiar? Yes, it's that dress again.

Every woman has her favourite outfit — the one that, whatever fashion dictates, is pulled out of the wardrobe again and again. And it is nice to know that the Princess of Wales is no different from the rest of us.

Yesterday on a visit to the London Lighthouse AIDS hospice in North Kensington she wore a crepe de chine dress in royal blue with a floral print. The dress, with a ruched waist and tulip sleeves was

By NEWBY HANDS

charming. But in fashion terms it was hardly new, as that longer, on-the-knee hemline proved. Indeed, Diana first wore it in public more than four years ago.

It was made for her by designer Bellville Sassoon for her 1988 Bicentennial trip to Australia. Since then she has worn it to polo at Smith's Lawn, on tours of Nigeria and Brazil and more recently in Seville.

For some women it would be a matter of make do and mend, but not for a Princess who has every designer clamouring to dress her. In her case it is all part of her

deliberate effort to shed that glossy clothes-horse image.

We first saw some of her hand-me-down' suits being worn by her sisters. Then a few old outfits began reappearing with clever adaptations. Frumpy peplums disappeared and hemlines were raised, often by the original designer. Jackets have also been re-cut to update an expensive ensemble.

But this dress must be a special favourite as it has survived unchanged through eight fashion seasons which have seen a rise then a sudden drop in hemlines.

Perhaps it has sentimental value. Or it could just be that blue is her favourite colour. Whatever the reason, it looks as good as ever.

The most frequently worn of all the Princess's dresses was this 1988 floral crêpe-de-Chine design, originally made for a foreign tour ABOVE Over a period of five years, from 1988 to 1992, it survived the vagaries of passing trends to be worn for everything from watching Polo at Smiths Lawn, Windsor to tours of Seville, Lagos and São Paolo, prompting the *Daily Mail* article, 21 July 1992 OPPOSITE Diana called it her "caring dress" and liked to wear it for her visits to hospitals and hospices, and especially to meet children who were attracted to the bright colours [Photograph Tim Graham © Getty Images]

1989

THIS PAGE, LEFT From romantic frills and ruffles to sexy sophistication: the Princess of Wales arrives for a 1993 film premiere in Bellville Sassoon's little black dress with beaded jewelled straps, one of the glamorous evening dresses that were auctioned at Christie's, New York in 1997 [Photograph Tim Graham, © Getty Images] ABOVE The original Bellville Sassoon sketch OPPOSITE PAGE The Princess backstage with members of the Kirov Ballet at the London Coliseum, 1993 [© PA Photos/Rebecca Naden]

nov.10ᵗʰ 1993.

ABOVE AND OPPOSITE PAGE A last-minute buy, the tartan jacket and black pencil skirt that Diana bought in the morning and wore later the same day to turn on the Bond Street Christmas lights, November 1993. The Princess often liked the immediacy of coming to the shop and choosing a dress or outfit from the rails [Photograph Jonathan Buckmaster. © Express Newspapers] OVERLEAF My last meeting with the Princess, at the London gala preview of her charity fashion auction, 'Dresses' in June 1997 [Photograph Tim Graham. © Getty Images]

BELLVILLE BRIDES- QUEEN FOR A DAY

'Those Wedding Bellvilles' *Women's Wear Daily* 25 May 1967. Illustration Steven Stipelman © Condé Nast Publications

BELLVILLE BRIDES — QUEEN FOR A DAY When I first arrived at Bellville, Belinda was in the process of making a wedding dress for her sister, Camilla. This was my introduction to that great Bellville speciality – making wonderful wedding dresses. As Belinda told *Women's Wear Daily* in 1965, "We love doing brides. It's the one time you can be completely impractical."[27] I realised I had joined a company which had the monopoly on society weddings. We made more dresses for society brides than any other British couturier, and our couture order books read like a cross between *Debrett's*, *Who's Who* and an excerpt from *Jennifer's Diary*.

In the early '60s, Bellville was famous for dressing debutantes, and these Bellville debs became Bellville brides – they were young and often adventurous couture enthusiasts. Soon weddings accounted for a good quarter of our business and once we had moved to Cadogan Lane in 1962, we had space for our own dedicated bridal workroom, which was unprecedented for a British couturier in the swinging '60s. Then demand began to come from other directions. Prestigious retailers, both in London and America, were interested in the new young British couture talent. The Bellville wholesale operation started in 1961 when we were invited to design a collection of ready-to-wear bridal dresses for London's most stylish department store, Woollands in Knightsbridge. That was followed by another invitation to design an exclusive wedding dress collection, this time for Bergdorf Goodman the famous fashion department store in New York.

At the same time, we were making couture wedding dresses for private clients all year round and our workrooms were always full to capacity. Brides have always come to us for these very grand English society weddings. An abbey or a cathedral was often the setting for a Bellville bride, who perhaps wore the family tiara and was photographed for the papers or the glossy magazines. The press certainly picked up on our society success. In 1960 the *Daily Mail* described us as the company that 'makes the prettiest, most feminine and original wedding dresses for the smartest, grandest and best-known weddings.'[28] In February 1965 a feature in *Woman's Journal* magazine began: 'The bride was dressed by Belinda Bellville…and that means that she's bound to be one of the most looked at, talked about, and best dressed brides of the year. Belinda Bellville brides always are. She's the society brides' own designer, their first choice when only the most beautiful dress in the world will do.'[29] In June 1963, Ernestine Carter, fashion editor of the *Sunday Times*, highlighted the Bellville bridal phenomenon with a feature on four of our eminent society brides: Lady Philippa Wallop, Candida Betjeman, Sarah Harmsworth, and Lindy Martineau. Under the headline, 'Wedding Belle', she reported that we had just finished our eightieth wedding dress of the season, with twenty more to finish by October![30]

Every bride wants to be a queen for the day – and she requires a dress that fulfils her dreams. The Bellville Sassoon style has always been intensely romantic, very elegant and feminine. If the bride liked the idea, we could also be quite dramatic – simple shapes given the deluxe treatment with sumptuous fabrics and lavish decoration. These dresses were great fun to do and Belinda and I always thrived on our wedding commissions. Today these 'Dream Dresses' remain a very important part of our business. It is the custom for a couture house to end each fashion show with a bridal gown – these are really inspirational suggestions, as hardly any bride-to-be chooses her wedding dress from the collection. What a bride wants is a dress that nobody else has ever seen, something special that is made just for her, something completely individual. These dresses

OPPOSITE Model Liese Deniz in 'Celeste', a '60s wedding dress in polka dotted net, with matching veil, that departed from tradition with a short balloon skirt and strapless bodice, 1960 [*Women's Wear Daily* © Condé Nast Publications]

are often the most extravagant things a designer can create. They are part romance, part fantasy – a fairy tale come true.

The secret of a perfect wedding dress is not just down to expert craftsmanship and the skill of the designer, it also relies on a combination of communication and intuition. The moment you first meet the bride-to-be is crucial, as you discover what she wants and how she wishes to see herself. Before you do anything else, you must gain her confidence so you can truly interpret her dream – whether it is a country wedding or a grand affair in an historic setting.

When designing a wedding dress several things have to be taken into consideration – not just the bride's requirements, but equally important are when and where the wedding is to take place. The dress must be right for the bride, but also for the venue and the ceremony. A grand dress with a long train simply will not work in a country church with a short and narrow aisle, and a minimalist dress, however lovely, would be lost in a great cathedral. I like a traditional wedding, and prefer off-whites like ivory and cream as I think they are much kinder and more flattering than pure white, which can look hard. I advise this overall soft theme, including for the flowers, because it is romantic as well as dramatic – both for the bride and her bridesmaids. You have to think of the picture as a whole, and contrasting colours can muddle and distract, whereas a look of dramatic simplicity underlines the beauty and significance of the occasion. Jewellery is also important, and we are often asked to incorporate a special piece. I think pearls always look lovely with a wedding dress and some brides are lucky enough to have the choice of a family tiara.

I frequently ask the bride and her family what they will say when they look at their photographs in five, or even ten years' time. A classic dress is always a beautiful dress in retrospect, even twenty years later, but sometimes fashion styles of the moment can become a pastiche of the period. A wedding dress should be breathtaking, but extreme styles are rarely successful because they date so quickly. This does not mean that designers are not influenced by current trends and Bellville Sassoon has always been a style leader in the bridal world. In fact, it is often the case that tradition can also be ultra-stylish. There is a certain nostalgia associated with bridal dresses – up-to-the-minute fashions look too stark and inappropriate. In the '60s, I remember young brides-to-be, typical Dolly birds and Chelsea girls, would come in wearing high boots and miniskirts, but every single one of them wanted a romantic wedding dress, often one that harked back to the Victorian or Edwardian era.

There are definite moods in bridal wear as with fashion in general. In 1981 the Princess of Wales' wedding dress revived the romantically extravagant crinoline. Then came wedding dresses with tight, boned bodices – the corset dresses, and then Thirties-style bias-cut satin slips. Through our love of historical costume, Bellville Sassoon helped to introduce a period look for wedding dresses as we were inspired by, and then reinterpreted, our favourite eras: Restoration, Empire, Victorian and Edwardian. Many of our brides are brought in to see us by their mothers, who were themselves originally Bellville brides. On one occasion a charming duchess and her daughter came in for a wedding dress with a special request. "I know this is a bit unusual," said the duchess, " But we'd like you to copy a relative's wedding dress." This caused some concern because we don't copy dresses. However, I suggested she show me a picture of the dress she had in mind and she agreed. A week later, a large limousine pulled up outside the shop. The duchess and her daughter came in, followed by a chauffeur carrying a huge gilt-framed portrait of her relative – by Gainsborough! It was no longer a problem – we designed and made our version of the dress and it was exquisite.

230

With my assistant, George Sharp, Lorcan and a 'bride' wearing a crinoline-style wedding dress from our 1993 collection

ABOVE Countess Leopold von Bismarck wears a Tudor inspired wedding dress, 1984 [By kind permission Countess Leopold von Bismarck] OPPOSITE Lady Sarah Curzon, one of Bellville's most beautiful society brides, radiant and romantic at her wedding to Piers Courage, 1966 [Photograph Lichfield. By kind permission Lady Sarah Aspinall] OVERLEAF LEFT One of our first ready-to-wear wedding dresses, featured in the *Sunday Times*, 1962 [Photograph David Olins] OVERLEAF RIGHT Charmian Montagu Douglas Scott, a notably fashionable bride wears Bellville Couture at her wedding to Archie Stirling, 1964.

231

THIS PAGE The full wedding procession, bride Dawn Wells with her retinue of bridesmaids and pages, all in Bellville Couture at her 1961 wedding, one of the first that I designed with Belinda [© Fashion Museum/Bath & North East Somerset Council] OPPOSITE PAGE Bellville bride Lady Philippa Wallop, daughter of the Earl and Countess of Portsmouth, arrives for her wedding to Viscount Chelsea, son of Earl Cadogan, with her hair swept up into an unusual toque of white raffia flowers embroidered with crystal drops, which matched the sleeves of her dress [*Queen*, June 5 1963. Photograph Norman Parkinson. © The Norman Parkinson Archive] OVERLEAF LEFT Society bride Lady Philippa Wallop, a fashion editor at *Harper's Bazaar*, chose Bellville Couture; her dress and train were offset by sleeves in white tulle embroidered with white raffia flowers and crystal drops [© Fashion Museum/Bath & North East Somerset Council] OVERLEAF RIGHT 'Wedding Belle', Candida Betjeman, daughter of poet John Betjeman, marries Rupert Lycett Green in Bellville Couture [© Fashion Museum/Bath & North East Somerset Council] Both these society brides, featured in the *Sunday Times* in June 1963, project a time when weddings were a matter of public spectacle and entertainment, as crowds gathered, with children at the forefront, and lined the bridal path to see the bride

234

For a bride the crowning glory is literally the veil and headdress. They are an integral part of the total look as they complete the image, so it is important that they enhance and never distract from the dress. For many brides, a simple flower headdress is enough, but some brides are fortunate enough to have a family lace veil, and often there is a tiara too. The security arrangements are such that we often never see the tiara until the morning of the wedding, when it goes straight up to the workroom to have the veil mounted and attached, which is an art in itself. Some of the jewellery we are invited to use is quite spectacular – brought round to us directly from the bank vault. As well as family tiaras, we sometimes work with precious family veils. If these are to be used, they need specialist handling and go off to the Royal School of Needlework to be carefully cleaned and, where necessary, repaired. The tradition of the bridal face veil goes back thousands of years, and there is even a mention in the Old Testament in the Bible: Jacob, having worked in the fields for seven years, lifts the wedding veil and finds he has married the wrong bride, Leah. He has to work another seven years before he is able to marry his intended, Leah's younger sister, Rachel. At Jewish weddings, it is therefore tradition for the groom's mother to lift the bride's veil to check that her son has got the right bride!

There are two things I always advise against. One is having masses of bridesmaids and pages – there is enough to think of on the day without having to supervise a host of over-excited or bored children. The other is inviting the prospective mother-in-law to the fittings. It is the designer's place to keep everything progressing smoothly and the success and confidence of the bride, as well as any other family members we may be dressing, is vital for keeping peace on the day. Of course, for the majority of brides, getting their dream wedding dress is a happy experience from start to finish. Throughout it all, whatever the obstacles and problems, I always endeavour to give the bride what she wants, and to pour oil on any troubled waters – sometimes you have to have the patience of a saint, the perception and insight of a psychologist, and the negotiating skills of a United Nations peacekeeping envoy!

Weddings can bring out the best and worst in human nature and over the years there have been a few dramas. I remember designing a very ornate dress for an Arab princess, who insisted that the train had to be twelve feet long. When it came to the final fitting, her lady-in-waiting brought out her own tape measure to check that the length was correct and we hadn't short-changed her! We made another richly decorated dress for a young Arab bride. Her mother chose the design, which was completely covered in pearl and crystal embroidery; the dress weighed a ton – the girl could hardly move in it. To protect all the precious embroidery, the dress was carefully packed in layer upon layer of tissue in a large box. The man who came to collect the dress refused to take it in its special packaging, and insisted on squashing it unceremoniously into a large carrier bag instead. The workroom ladies, who had spent months of painstaking work completing all the embroidery and then pressing it perfectly for its journey abroad, told me they felt like weeping. Some brides just can't make up their minds. One beautiful Russian bride who was marrying an oligarch had two completely different couture wedding dresses made and flew both dresses out to Moscow, as she couldn't decide which style she preferred!

Times have changed and there are now so many registry office weddings that a lot of the traditional rules on dressing the bride are disregarded. One of the biggest changes in the design of wedding dresses is their relative nudity – they are barer now than they have ever been. Even in the permissive seventies the bride covered her shoulders for the ceremony; now a strapless dress is quite acceptable. However, many brides will wear a strapless dress but cover up with a co-ordinating bolero, shrug or lace fichu for the ceremony in the church or synagogue. Today,

with the concept of the wedding as spectacle, almost theatre, the wedding dress seems to be styled as much for the wedding party as it is for the actual wedding ceremony. For me, the irony is that weddings have come full circle as there is a real revival of the aspirational grand-scale English society wedding, which is now reinterpreted and adapted for every level, every taste, every budget, with an historic house standing in for a cathedral or abbey, an elaborate wedding dress for the bride and a host of bridesmaids and pages, and an equally lavish reception – almost just as it was when I designed my first Bellville wedding dresses back in the late '50s. Today, however, the bride is just as likely to be marrying a premier league footballer as a viscount or duke, and the wedding may have been sponsored by a celebrity magazine, which may have participated in a bidding war to cover the occasion or she may be paying for it herself.

Nevertheless, despite all the changes some wedding traditions do remain. In the early days, until the mid-seventies, it was a Bellville tradition to give each bride a blue garter. Now, to make sure the bride wears the essential "something blue", we sew a tiny blue bow inside the bodice. Then there are the superstitions that dressmakers have passed down to each generation – sewing a hair into the hem of the wedding dress is one of them so that the dressmaker, too, will marry. Practicalities have to be thought of, and tricks of the trade include stitching rows of gathered net frills on the underside of the train so that it glides gracefully and smoothly down the aisle. Brides enjoy the ritual of getting dressed in their dream dress, seeing themselves transformed, and are often quite clear about what they do and do not want. Brides love handcrafted detail like intricate bead embroidery, and they also love lots of tiny covered buttons and loop fastenings down the back of a dress – far more interesting and seductive than a zip. Brides like the idea that someone has to help them into the dress – and later, help them out of it!

There are two distinct schools of thought when it comes to the dream dress. There are those brides who will go to any lengths to look their best, and then there are those for whom comfort comes first, and fashion second. (One recent bride even wore silver trainers under her wedding dress!) To every bride I say, "This is the day to forget comfort, dear – you can suffer afterwards, but for your starring moment you're going to look beautiful!" For most women, their wedding day is their most glamorous moment ever. Their priority must be to look their absolute best. All brides strive to lose weight – they usually want to drop a whole dress size – and we are constantly having to take the dress in at fittings. They've dieted, they've exercised, they've starved, no sweets or chocolate, no favourite food treats, they've fretted and worried – they've done it – and they'll probably never look this good again!

The final fitting is always the most reassuring and rewarding for everyone concerned. Apart from the delight of the bride-to-be, there is another memorable feature which can be both striking and moving – the "Aah" moment – the instant when a parent sees their daughter dressed as the bride. Of course, when you start off with a bride-to-be who is already very attractive, you are halfway there. Most rewarding for me, however, is someone who is perhaps not so overtly glamorous because I know I can really help and guide her. I can transform her into her dream so that she too looks beautiful, and that is the task of the wedding dress. All the elements have to come together and reflect glory on the bride. Funnily enough, I have noticed that it's not the mothers – who have been there throughout the process and seen the evolution through all the fittings – who shed a tear, but the fathers who get very emotional on seeing "my little girl" in her beautiful dress. Mothers cry at the ceremony, fathers cry at the final fitting. My moment comes when I see the bride in her dress, complete with headdress and veil – and I know I have made her a princess for the day.

os-style wedding dress in silk georgette, with a close-fitting headdress and veil, lushly trimmed in lace,

gue Brides, September 1973. Photograph Barry Lategan/*Vogue*. © The Condé Nast Publications Ltd]

OPPOSITE PAGE Belinda's daughter, Polly Whately, now
Viscountess Coke in a neoclassical-style wedding dress,
December 1996. Belinda was thrilled to help design her
youngest daughter's wedding dress THIS PAGE Minimalist
bride, Felicia von Pallandt, 1999, in the simple flattery of a
bias-cut satin slip wedding dress, '90s style.

Bellville Brides THIS PAGE Contemporary-style bride in a strapless net dress with a traditional tiara, January 2006 OPPOSITE PAGE The Edwardian-bride – white wild silk wedding dress with pie-frilled ruffles, January 2007 [Photographs Iain Philpott/*You and Your Wedding* © The National Magazine Company]

Sketches from the Bellville Sassoon wedding portfolio TOP ROW LEFT TO RIGHT From Bellville et Cie, high necks and long sleeves for the demure '60s bride; the empire line with lace train; lace bridal coat with hood; the flamenco bride; at Bellville Sassoon, the medieval influenced '70s style. BOTTOM ROW LEFT TO RIGHT The '80s rose–trimmed bustled bride; the body-conscious bride; the fishtail hem replaces the train; the sleeveless wedding dress and the cover-up bolero; bare shoulders and bustle back with lace underskirt; off-the-shoulder glamour noughties style.

JEWELS AND BALLS

Shakira Caine and Merrill Thomas, both in Bellville Sassoon at the opening of Zandra Rhodes's Fashion and Textile Museum, London 2004.

JEWELS AND BALLS At Bellville Sassoon we undoubtedly have the frocks to go with the rocks and over the years I have certainly seen some magnificent jewellery. The British aristocracy, I have discovered, may plead poverty but then produce their impressive family heirlooms. These jewels can provide the tiara for the bride, and sparkling diamonds for the belle of the ball. For the grandest balls and parties we are frequently asked to design a dress to complement these family jewels, which can be exceptional. Everyone thinks of the British woman as all tweeds and twinsets, but she really shines at night – and often has amazing jewellery.

These occasions undeniably, both then and now, have a sense of theatre. The combination and effect of so many beautiful women in stunning dresses and glittering jewels in one place at one time will always attract the headlines and have an impact round the world. Belinda's first customers were London's young debutantes for whom she made those wonderful balldresses that graced all the pages of the society magazines. After I arrived, making these beautiful dresses for the grand occasion became our speciality – and brought us an international clientele. As the press picked up on our increasingly successful profile, very soon our reputation was truly international and for every major ball both at home and abroad, flocks of fashionable women came to us for something extra-special.

It was always a challenge to balance the needs of the avalanche of titled customers all wanting dresses for the same exclusive events: The Wilton Ball, the Holkham Ball, the Windsor Ball, the Blenheim Ball, and so on. The constant factor at all these balls was not only the dresses, but the dazzling jewellery. Once the dresses were complete, the jewels would arrive on the scene. As the English couturier, Hardy Amies memorably quoted about the French, "[They] have the frocks, but the British have the rocks!"[31]

Some of the most magnificent jewels that ever entered our premises were the famed Indian jewels presented to Lord and Lady Mountbatten when they were appointed the last Viceroy and Vicereine of India in the late 1940s. We were making a dress for Lady Pamela Hicks (née Mountbatten) to wear to Princess Margaret's wedding in 1960. It was one of the last occasions when royal guests wore elaborate long dresses for the morning ceremony and these dresses required suitably grand decoration. The Mountbatten jewels were priceless and precious enough to need the security guard who accompanied Lady Pamela's husband the interior decorator, David Hicks, to the fitting.

Much of the jewellery that we saw had a romantic history and an aristocratic pedigree, like that belonging to Nicolette, Lady Londonderry, a noted society beauty of the '60s, who was one of our couture clients. She owned the fabled Londonderry jewels, which included a magnificent amethyst and diamond necklace and superb diamond drop earrings. These jewels were originally given to Frances Anne, Marchioness of Londonderry as a love gift by the hopelessly smitten Tsar Alexander I of Russia in 1814. Another of my favourite clients wanted me to design a dress for her to wear with an equally unique piece of jewellery, which she brought to the fitting in its original velvet case. When she opened the case it revealed a necklace of sapphires, and I saw each one was carved with an inscription on the back – the necklace was a gift to Queen Marie Antoinette from Louis XVI of France.

THIS PAGE The first of my designs ever to be featured in a magazine, worn by debutante Miss Alexandra Versen: a typical deb's balldress in 'pink champagne moiré with white ribbon-embroidered tulle for the bodice and sloping dust ruffle, very high in the front with a pie-frill bodice, 62gns.' [Queen, 3 February 1959. Photograph Brien Kirley. © The National Magazine Company] OVERLEAF Couture luxury: two Bellville et Cie ballgowns modelled by Liese Deniz typify the late '50s, when long white gloves and high style formality were all the fashion. The dress on the left with its deep tiers of satin organza, was called 'Himalaya' [Photyograph Michel Molinare]

Beautiful jewels have always been given as love tokens. One overheard conversation between two of our clients at the Bellville showroom in the '60s sums up the absolute appeal of jewellery to a woman's soul. The conversation had turned to the merits of certain husbands and fiancés. One customer turned to the other and said, "But my dear, why ever are you marrying him? He's already got one foot in the grave." The other customer smiled knowingly. "Yes darling", she replied, "but the other foot's in Cartier!"

Clients often want us to create a dress around a particular piece of jewellery and dealing with such valuable jewels brings its own security problems, but customers get round these in novel ways. In the early '60s we made a pink gazar dress for Lady O, which was specifically for her to wear with her pink diamond necklace. We asked to see the necklace so that we could get the neckline exactly right and she promised to bring it to the following fitting. When she next appeared, however, there was no sign of the necklace. "Oh no, I couldn't bring it because of the insurance," Lady O explained, "It costs so much to get it out of the bank – so I did this instead," she added, pointing to the blue biro mark she had drawn all around her neck to show where the neckline should go.

On another occasion, a great Scottish society beauty, a Countess, wanted an evening dress to wear with her magnificent Edwardian deep stomacher belt, which was made entirely from diamonds. This precious item was kept at her jewellers and she asked Belinda and I if we would go and see it there. The Countess wasn't sure if she should wear any other jewellery with this dramatic piece, "While you're there," she added, "Just ask to see my diamond earrings." So off Belinda and I went to Garrards, the royal jewellers. Up from the vaults came a large red leather trunk embossed with a gold heraldic crest. When the trunk was unlocked we saw umpteen sets of drawers, each one embossed with a letter corresponding to the jewels within – 'D' for diamonds, 'E' for emeralds, 'R' for rubies, and so on. Remembering the Countess's instruction, we asked to see her diamond earrings. "Of course," replied the man from Garrards, "Which ones? The Countess has twenty-two pairs!"

Then there was the case of the supermarket plastic bag which Lady R brought to us so that we could design a very special dress for a very special ball. When Lady R tipped out the

MORE DEBUT-IFUL PEOPLE

Min Aspinall (Thea Porter)

Hon. Roso Lambton (Belinda Bellville)

Emma Soames (Belinda Bellville)

Hon. Kerena Mond (Gina Fratini)

Sarah Giles (Belinda Bellville)

Lady Sarah Crichton-Stuart (Thea Porter)

The Ballroom Queen

VISCOUNTESS CRANBOURNE · COUNTESS OF DALKEITH · MRS. JOCELYN STEVENS · BELINDA BELLVILLE · LADY PORCHESTER · SASHA ALEXANDRA PHILLIPS · LADY PAMELA HICKS · MRS. HAROLD PHILLIPS · LADY ANNE TENNANT

THE BALLROOM QUEEN . . . Belinda Bellville — the blond Belgravian who is the darling of London's young beauties — scoops the creme of London's Young Gentlewomen for the ball of the year at Luton Hoo, historic home of Lady Zia Wernher, for the coming-out of her granddaughter, 18-year-old Sasha Alexandra Phillips . . . most of the British royal family was there, and a whole bevy of foreign royals . . . The message from Luton Hoo: Clear slim shapes with ostrich, flower and bead trimmings to offset dazzling precious heirloom jewelry.

Drawings by Anneliese

Two *Women's Wear Daily* articles hail Bellville as the reigning label of London's young rich set OPPOSITE PAGE 'More Debut-iful People', 27 June 1969 and THIS PAGE 'The Ballroom Queen', 1964 [pp 256–257 *Women's Wear Daily*. Illustrations by Anneliese. © The Condé Nast Publications Inc] OVERLEAF The Bellville balldress '60s style – a slimmer silhouette with the high empire line bodice, delicate lace and embroidery

Prado.

Opaline.

contents of the plastic bag there was a large velvet jewel box containing a demi-parure, a set of amazing jewels. There was a necklace of emeralds the size of gull's eggs set in diamonds, with an even larger pendant stone – the necklace was so huge it resembled a mayoral chain, and there were bracelets and earrings to match. Looking at these jewels, Lady R confessed, "I don't really like them – and I've got a red set, too." Explaining her lack of enthusiasm, she added, " I feel they could be by Butler and Wilson if you didn't know the difference!"

One of our grandest and most beautiful clients was Queen Noor of Jordan. On one particular occasion in the early '80s she came to our shop in Pavilion Road to fit several dresses she had ordered. Queen Noor arrived accompanied by a rather butch-looking female security guard. The guard sat astride an antique wooden chest we had by the door in which we stored our carrier bags, with legs akimbo looking rather menacing. Disconcertingly, she wouldn't let anyone else into the shop, and kept her right hand permanently in her large handbag, and we realised she must have a gun inside the bag. When the fitting was over, we found that Queen Noor had left behind her necklace, a large gold pendant which had an Arabic inscription, possibly from the Koran, picked out in diamonds. We rang up to explain the situation and the same security guard, this time with a genial smile, returned to collect the jewel.

One customer who liked to mix precious antique jewellery with the cheap and cheerful was a glamorous figure on the social scene in the '60s and '70s. Anne Fleming, the beautiful wife of James Bond creator Ian Fleming, came to us for many of her couture dresses. She had some fabulous pearls with a beautiful Georgian diamond clasp in the centre, which she always wore except when they were being re-strung, when, instead, she would wear a necklace of white plastic 'Poppet' beads that simply clipped together! At the other extreme, another client's dress was designed around a necklace so valuable that we had to do the final fitting with the necklace in a huge steel bank vault – it was like a scene from a James Bond film.

In the '50s, when I first began working with Belinda, there was a great deal of emphasis on grand parties and balls and the grandest of these were the themed costume balls. Hosts and guests alike made the effort to 'dress' for the occasion, and sometimes preparations were lavish in the extreme. I particularly remember making some exquisite dresses for a Rothschild Ball in Paris. The theme of this ball was Marcel Proust, and we made a number of romantic *belle époque* dresses for our customers. Belinda and I were in our element as it was a period that we particularly loved and the dresses we designed greatly influenced the next collection we did. The whole *fin-de-siècle* era was such a stylish and over-the-top period for women's fashion. It has always been my favourite era, and once again the elegant portrait of Lady Sassoon by Sargent, which had fascinated me since my childhood, came to mind and it became an important inspiration for the mood of the dresses we designed.

Cecil Beaton, the socialite aesthete and eminent photographer of his day, described the Proust ball as "The Party of Any Year". Hosted by the Baron and Baronne Guy de Rothschild it was held in December 1971 to celebrate the centenary of the birth of the famous French novelist. This glamorous event had such an élite profile that it was extensively covered by both British and French *Vogue*, as well as America's influential *Women's Wear Daily*, and the *Sunday Times*.[12] British *Vogue* commissioned Beaton to bring the ball to life for its readers, and devoted a six-page spread to his feature.[13] This was one of the last great costume balls and Marie-Hélène de Rothschild, the queen of Paris society at this time, spared no expense. There was a sit-down dinner for 350 guests, and a buffet supper for 350 more, held at the Rothschilds' impressive nineteenth-century

chateau, Ferrières, just outside Paris. The dramatic grandeur of the occasion was apparent even before the guests entered the chateau as miles of flaming torches guided them to their destination.

Everyone certainly entered into the *belle époque* spirit and couturiers in Paris, London and Rome were kept busy creating extravagant Proustian costumes. For Lady Annabel Birley, now Lady Annabel Goldsmith, we made a beautiful dress in pale lime green taffeta. As sister to Lord Londonderry, she was able to accessorise the dress with the fabulous family jewels, which were worth a king's ransom. Like the other guests she didn't travel light – she took with her a maid, her hairdresser – and two security guards. Lady Annabel still has very vivid memories of her special outfit. "God, that dress was amazing. Even though I say it myself, it did look a knockout at the ball – I was anxious to show my aristocratic lineage and was literally smothered in the Londonderry jewels, most of which were given to my great great grandmother by the Tsar of Russia. I wore the tiara, which is bigger than the Queen's, accompanied by a diamond necklace and a stomacher of diamonds and pearls which hung down the middle of the dress. Of course, it was completely over the top but guaranteed to impress the French, in particular Marie-Hélène de Rothschild who gave the ball."[34]

We also made extravagant taffeta dresses for Princess Loewenstein and for Lady Sarah Courage, but my favourite dress was the one we made for Lady Beatty, who had modelled for us at Bellville. She chose an Edwardian style in pale orchid pink taffeta, which was photographed by Beaton, appearring as the opening image of his *Vogue* feature. Lady Beatty's dress was variously pintucked, pleated, and ruffled and for extra authenticity, we even managed to find a Victorian cutting machine to give the rosettes that decorated the bodice and neckline a serated edge using the original tools. The *Sunday Times* reported: 'David Sassoon of Bellville Sassoon is dressmaker to the young Establishment… the ruffles are in Mr Sassoon's best vein.'[35]

It was an extraordinary night. As well as a bevy of Bellville Sassoons for the London contingent, there were dresses by Yves Saint Laurent, Dior, Lanvin, and Courrèges. Salvador Dali rubbed shoulders with Her Serene Highness Princess Grace of Monaco. The Duchess of Windsor wore blue satin by Givenchy, while Elizabeth Taylor, in black taffeta and lace by Valentino, wore a fortune in emeralds and diamonds. The most dramatic outfit of the evening undoubtedly belonged to Marisa Berenson, the socialite granddaughter of the couturière Schiaparelli, who appeared as the Marchesa Casati in a striking black ensemble designed by Visconti's costume designer, Piero Tosi, who had obviously been inspired by the imposing Boldini portrait which now belongs to Lord Lloyd Webber. I have always admired the costumes designed by Piero Tosi – he captured so perfectly the mood of the Victorian and Edwardian periods for films like *The Leopard*, *Mayerling* and *Death in Venice*. I identify with the strong romantic theme in these films, and find his style very inspiring – he has certainly influenced many of my collections.

I could remember seeing the Marchesa Casati as an old lady in London. When I was a student at the Royal College of Art in the '50s I was fascinated by the sight of the Marchesa shopping at Harrods or walking in Knightsbridge. In broad daylight she would be dressed head-to-toe in original *belle époque* costume: tight hobble skirt and high-necked, fitted peplum jacket, gloves, buttoned boots, and a hat, with her face powdered white. Everyone would stop and stare – it is amazing how some women remain in a time warp of their youth.

Designs for the Proust Ball, Paris 1971 OPPOSITE PAGE Lady Beatty in our *belle époque* dress, and THIS PAGE Three Bellville Sassoon Proust Ball designs as featured in *Women's Wear Daily* [pp262-263 *Women's Wear Daily*, 2 December, 1971 © The Condé Nast Publications Inc.]

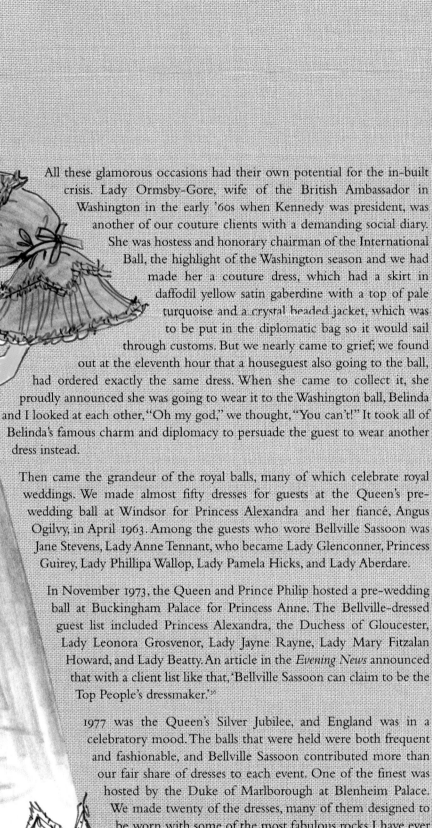

All these glamorous occasions had their own potential for the in-built crisis. Lady Ormsby-Gore, wife of the British Ambassador in Washington in the early '60s when Kennedy was president, was another of our couture clients with a demanding social diary. She was hostess and honorary chairman of the International Ball, the highlight of the Washington season and we had made her a couture dress, which had a skirt in daffodil yellow satin gaberdine with a top of pale turquoise and a crystal beaded jacket, which was to be put in the diplomatic bag so it would sail through customs. But we nearly came to grief; we found out at the eleventh hour that a houseguest also going to the ball, had ordered exactly the same dress. When she came to collect it, she proudly announced she was going to wear it to the Washington ball, Belinda and I looked at each other, "Oh my god," we thought, "You can't!" It took all of Belinda's famous charm and diplomacy to persuade the guest to wear another dress instead.

Then came the grandeur of the royal balls, many of which celebrate royal weddings. We made almost fifty dresses for guests at the Queen's pre-wedding ball at Windsor for Princess Alexandra and her fiancé, Angus Ogilvy, in April 1963. Among the guests who wore Bellville Sassoon was Jane Stevens, Lady Anne Tennant, who became Lady Glenconner, Princess Guirey, Lady Phillipa Wallop, Lady Pamela Hicks, and Lady Aberdare.

In November 1973, the Queen and Prince Philip hosted a pre-wedding ball at Buckingham Palace for Princess Anne. The Bellville-dressed guest list included Princess Alexandra, the Duchess of Gloucester, Lady Leonora Grosvenor, Lady Jayne Rayne, Lady Mary Fitzalan Howard, and Lady Beatty. An article in the *Evening News* announced that with a client list like that, 'Bellville Sassoon can claim to be the Top People's dressmaker.'[36]

1977 was the Queen's Silver Jubilee, and England was in a celebratory mood. The balls that were held were both frequent and fashionable, and Bellville Sassoon contributed more than our fair share of dresses to each event. One of the finest was hosted by the Duke of Marlborough at Blenheim Palace. We made twenty of the dresses, many of them designed to be worn with some of the most fabulous rocks I have ever seen. Perhaps the pinnacle of these celebrations was the Gala held at Covent Garden, which certainly enchanted *Women's Wear Daily*: 'It was definitely the glamour evening of Jubilee week as England's stately country set trotted out their twinkliest family tiaras, their chunkiest brooches and bracelets, and their lengthiest ropes of pearls in honour of the Queen's Jubilee Gala at Covent Garden.'[37]

We designed dresses for the most exclusive and prestigious balls, but we didn't usually attend them ourselves. However, there were exceptions. In May 1966, we made dresses for a particularly important debutante. Eighteen-year-old Angela Nevill was one of the Queen's goddaughters, and Belinda and her husband and I were invited to her coming-out party, held at St James's Palace. There was a guest list of 900, headed by the Queen and Princess Margaret. We also designed dresses for many of the guests – we were particularly in demand as we had recently had a lot of press about the evening dresses we had made for Princess Margaret's American tour the previous autumn. The invitation stated 'decorations'. I knew that Belinda's husband, David would be wearing his army medals, and I also knew that Belinda would be looking amazing. I decided I had to wear my own 'decoration'; I remembered I had a bronze high jump medal from my school days and I wore this on a ribbon round my neck to tease Belinda. Belinda took one look at me, giggled then said, "For goodness' sake, David, take it off at once!" Apart from the small hiccup with my outfit, the main excitement for me was Belinda's gown, which we designed together – a long black organza Empire-style dress with a very low plunging neckline and enormous white organza ruffled sleeves that burst out from the shoulder like the centre of a peony. With this she wore a stunning Art Deco diamond necklace that had belonged to her grandmother, 'Cuckoo' Leith, which sat perfectly within the contour of the neckline. When Belinda entered the ballroom there was a definite stir of admiration and my real pleasure that evening was seeing how spectacular she looked – David and I were very proud to be her escorts. Jane Stevens looked divine in Bellville, and Belinda and I were delighted when we saw that Princess Margaret was also looking very glamorous – in our pink gazar dress that she had worn at the White House.

The social world of the couturier in the '60s had its exciting and dramatic moments. One of the most exciting fashion balls of this decade was given by Jerry Silverman and Shannon Rogers, two American designers – whatever they did they were larger than life. They had a penchant for throwing elaborate balls in opulent surroundings, having previously hosted parties in Venice and at Versailles. This time the venue for the ball was the Brighton Pavilion and they hired the Brighton Belle steam train to transport their guests there. The guests at the Brighton Pavilion Ball in August 1966 included some of London's most famous faces; anyone who was anyone in the fashion world was there, including Mary Quant and her husband Alexander Plunket Greene, Vidal Sassoon, Barbara Hulanicki, and Jean Muir, and the excitement started even before we had arrived. At Victoria station a red carpet the full length of the platform led us in style to the train. Once onboard, a gypsy orchestra played and champagne flowed freely. I was travelling to the ball with a group of friends, including fellow designer, Gerald McCann, who was wearing a very exotic-looking jewelled belt. Another passenger, emboldened by several glasses of champagne, made fun of the buckle, "What on earth are you wearing that ridiculous paste belt for?" he scoffed, "It just looks tacky." Gerald, who could be quite outrageous, took exception to this criticism. Bending forward, he removed the man's glasses, and then with his buckle he etched a deep groove around the edge of one of the lenses. That "tacky paste belt" was, as Gerald then informed us, an original by the Art Nouveau artist, Alphonse Mucha – and the diamonds were real!

Gerald wasn't the only one who had dressed for the occasion. I had been to Biba to get something special to wear. It was always fun to go shopping at Biba, no-one else had that look – it was a very exciting concept. I knew Barbara Hulanicki early on, when the first Biba was in Abingdon Road. I found something ideal for the ball – a white piqué woman's jacket. It fitted

me perfectly and I wore it tuxedo-style over black trousers – I thought I looked the bee's knees and felt I would definitely stand out in the crowd. When we arrived at the party the centrepiece was an enormous cake made in the form of the Brighton Pavilion. As I was admiring it, a guest approached me and asked me to bring him a glass of champagne. He had mistaken me for a waiter – I was absolutely mortified – and furious!

In 1972, Belinda and I were invited to participate in a big gala charity fashion show hosted by Mrs William McAlpine, with HSH Princess Grace of Monaco as guest-of-honour. Grace Kelly, as she had once been, was one of my fashion icons. I had always loved seeing her in the Hitchcock films *Rear Window*, *To Catch a Thief* and *Dial M for Murder*, and now I would be seeing and speaking to her in person. But meeting her shattered all my illusions. When we were introduced and I told her, "I've always been a great fan of yours", she reacted with what I can only describe as a glacial expression of absolute disinterest. "How kind," she replied very grandly, and moved on. It was a terrible disappointment – Grace wasn't very gracious after all!

Sometimes a customer will come in with a very specific dress or theme in mind and if I think it is a good idea I will do as the customer asks. In 1978 Pamela, Lady Harlech asked us to design a Ginger Rogers-style long white chiffon dress for a party she was giving to celebrate her husband, Lord Harlech's 60th birthday. Among the 300 guests were Jackie Onassis, Princess Alexandra and the Duchess of Devonshire. The indefatigable Pamela looked wonderful and *Vogue* reported that, appropriately, she danced the night away![38]

When the 1980s arrived, the lavish themed costume balls of the '50s, '60s, and '70s disappeared. People stopped hosting private balls, and in their place came the large-scale charity event. The economic boom of the '80s brought a wave of new city money, especially in London and America, and high-profile charity events became the latest way to channel the new excess. Apart from their good works, the good news for couturiers, was that they provided the perfect excuse to dress up, and glamorous dressing was right back at the top of the agenda.

These charity balls have become some of the most dazzling and eagerly anticipated social events of our time. One of my favourite clients and a good friend is Blaine Trump, the American socialite and philanthropist, who is frequently on the international Best Dressed List. I have regularly dressed Blaine for the annual Metropolitan Museum of Art Costume Institute Gala, which is one of the biggest social events in New York. The international guest list comprises the great, the good, and the super-chic. These glamorous, high-status gatherings are occasions that really require an attention-grabbing gown. Blaine never fails to sparkle at these events and she is a favourite of the paparazzi and the magazine photographers who are always looking for the most stylish guests.

In Britain, it is Elton John's extravagantly themed annual charity ball that is the highlight of the charity calendar. Shakira Caine, wife of the actor Michael Caine, is another favourite client, whom I love to design for, and she always looks stunning at such events. She has an inborn serene beauty and grace. She knows exactly what suits her, and her modelling background has given her an understanding of how to wear and move in a sophisticated evening dress. I have designed many of these for her to wear at various glamorous occasions, including the Oscars ceremonies, numerous international film premieres, and charity events.

Now, alongside, the ubiquitous charity ball, there is another contemporary re-working of old-school glamour. There has been a revival of the deb ball, with modern-day debutantes launched

The seductive silhouette: figure-hugging ruched net dress fit for the red carpet appearance

into society at the annual Crillon Ball in Paris. This is an international affair with daughters of British and European aristocracy mingling with the daughters of conspicuous new money. As the established Parisian houses like Dior and Chanel once more embrace the excesses of the past in designing for this new young clientele, they have been joined by newer names like Lacroix, Jean Paul Gaultier, and the Armani Privé label. Alongside these French and Italian couturiers, at Bellville Sassoon we also design dresses for this revival. This youth-orientated opulence fuses old traditions and new styles, as well as old and new money, just as I did in my earliest Bellville days when I was designing for various young Honourables and creamy-skinned debs like Miss Alexandra Versen.

Today, there is a fresh focus on glamour and a new arena for glamorous dressing – the red carpet has become the international celebrity catwalk. A phrase has even been coined to describe this phenomenon: red-carpet dressing. Young starlets and established actresses alike seek to prove their credentials on the red carpet where the public and the media are as interested in what they wear and how they look as they are by whether they win an award or not. It is a return to the golden days of Hollywood glamour as stars seek to outdo one another. The Hollywood Oscar ceremonies, along with the Golden Globes, the Venice Film Festival and the Cannes Film Festival have become some of the biggest venues for fashionable glamour, with the emphasis on contemporary couture and unique vintage. It is an exercise in sartorial one-upmanship and ultra-style exclusivity as the stars' stylists fight to search for the exceptional dress that will set off their own careers as much as that of the star who will be wearing it. Glamour is back with a capital 'G', but for Bellville Sassoon it never went away.

271

OPPOSITE PAGE Pink satin balldress with tulle underskirt, which featured in a photoshoot by Mario Testino for British *Vogue*, December 2001 THIS PAGE British actress Kelly Brook, recently voted the world's most beautiful woman, signals the return of the golden age of Hollywood glamour wearing Bellville Sassoon on the red carpet LEFT Attending the Prince's Trust Gala in London, November 2006 [Photograph Mark Stewart/Camera Press] RIGHT At the Cannes Film Festival, May 2006 [Photograph Chris Ashford/Camera Press] OVERLEAF LEFT Blaine Trump, in scarlet satin bustier dress, seen here with Princess Marie-Chantal of Greece, chooses Bellville Sassoon to make maximum impact at the Metropolitan Museum of Art Costume Institute Ball, New York, December 1995 [Photograph and © Patrick McMullan] OVERLEAF RIGHT Blaine Trump in a bottle green velvet bustier and Black Watch tartan taffeta skirt that fans out into a dramatic train at the Metropolitan Museum of Art Costume Institute Ball, New York, December 1994 [Photograph and © Patrick McMullan]

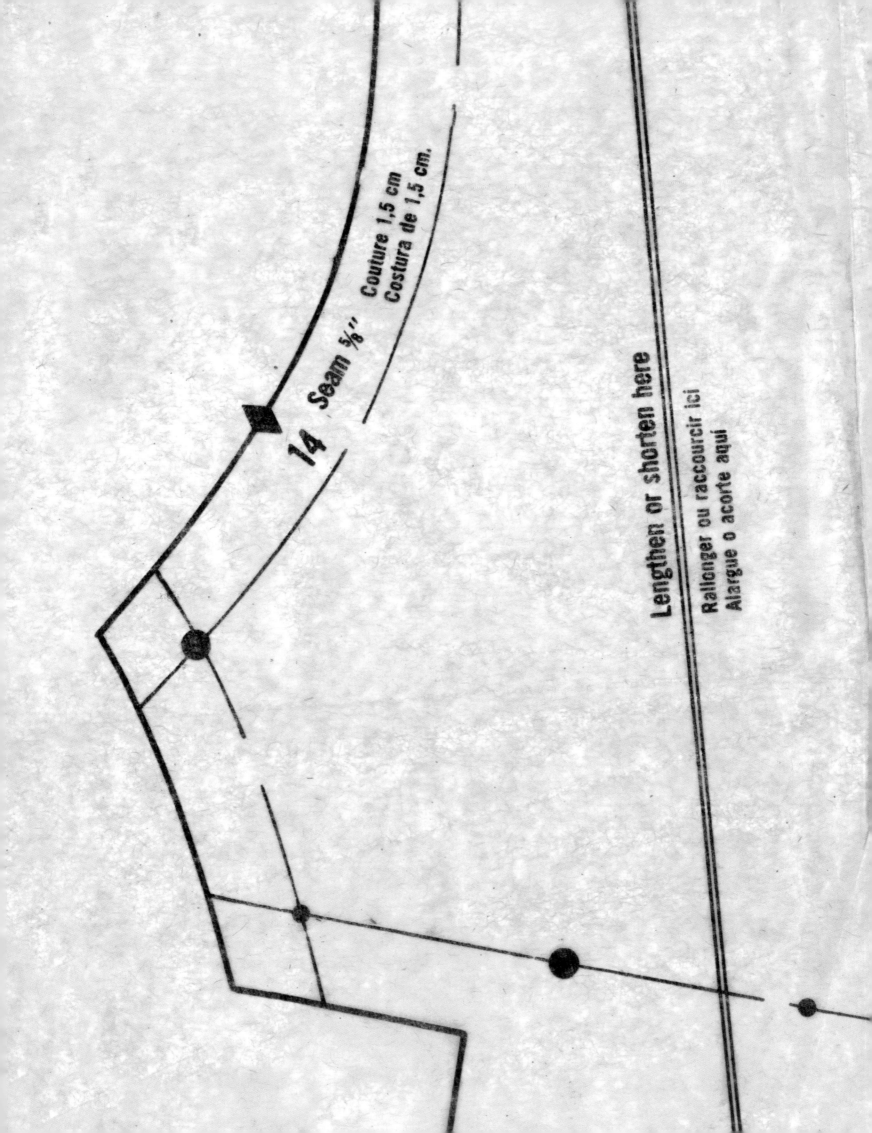

14 Seam 5/8"

Couture 1,5 cm
Costura de 1,5 cm.

Lengthen or shorten here

Rallonger ou raccourcir ici
Alargue o acorte aqui

7

Skirt Front
Jupe devant
Frente de la falda

Underline
Entoiler de triplure
Refuerzo

VOGUE PATTERN
Couturier Design
2112 Size 10
9 Pieces

VOGUE®
PATTERNS

VOGUE PATTERNS All fashion companies need an additional financial string to their bow, especially if they wish to survive in the long-term. Fashion remains a highly competitive business and licences provide important revenue for any company. Typically, many diversify with perfume, cosmetics, home collections, and the ever-important accessories: bags, shoes, sunglasses, scarves and jewellery; but it may be a surprise to learn that designer paper patterns can be just as significant.

Like other designers, we made our name with our couture and ready-to-wear collections, but there is another part of the business of which I am equally proud, which caters to a quite different group of customers. For over forty years we have had an extremely successful association with Vogue Patterns, the world's leading dress-pattern company, a singular achievement for a London label. Mostly known for its European and American designers, few British names have ever been featured (previously Jean Muir and more recently Betty Jackson) and today we are Vogue Patterns' only remaining British designers. Our patterns are sold all over the world and have added significantly to our success. While some designer brands have built empires on almost everything but clothes, many others like ourselves have built part of our business on giving the home dressmaker access to 'couture' designs.

In 1965 Belinda and I were making a name for ourselves on both sides of the Atlantic as London's new youthful couturiers, when we were approached by the Vogue Pattern company wishing to purchase designs from our couture collection. At this time Vogue Patterns had licences with many of the leading fashion houses in Paris and Italy, so we felt privileged to join this exciting and prestigious venture. We had just launched our ready-to-wear Boutique collection, but it was our reputation for couture evening and occasion wear, including our wedding dresses, that attracted the fashion scouts from Vogue Patterns.

In the '60s virtually every home had a sewing machine and home dressmaking was an extremely popular leisure activity. The latest Paris and Rome Collection trends, and increasingly home-grown design talent, provided the inspiration for home dressmakers who strove to interpret the new looks. Then as now, women took great pride in overcoming the challenges of a complicated pattern and enjoyed the craft of dressmaking, as well as a sense of achievement when they saw, and wore, the finished results. It was also the era of the local dressmaker, 'the little woman round the corner' who could be relied upon to whip up a cocktail or party dress at reasonable cost – with the help of a *Vogue* pattern.

Unlike today, dressmaking was then part of the school curriculum, regarded as a key domestic skill, and schoolgirls everywhere were taught how to hand stitch and use a sewing machine. For many this proved to be a useful practical skill, which in time enhanced their social life – in a few hours on a Saturday they could make a simple shift dress to wear that evening.

For those on smaller incomes, particularly teenagers, students and young adults, making one's own clothes meant they could afford versions of the new boutique trends which would otherwise be completely inaccessible. Even famous model Twiggy, the "Face of '66" and a style icon who became an international brand with her own fashion line, revealed that she had used *Vogue* patterns as a young home dressmaker, "By the time I was thirteen I was making my own clothes…Breaktimes [at school] would be spent discussing what we were going to wear that weekend. Some of us pooled our money in order to buy *Vogue* patterns which, although expensive, could be easily adapted if you knew how. And I knew how. Learning to sew was just part of growing up."[39]

OPPOSITE PAGE Home dressmaking at its most glamorous – a striking draped satin dress – a Bellville Sassoon style for Vogue Patterns. Since 1965, Bellville Sassoon has been designing for the increasingly chic demands of the international designer paper pattern market [Photograph © The McCall Pattern Company]

Not only in certain areas of Britain, but for countries like Australia and New Zealand, and even parts of America, large department stores hardly existed, let alone boutiques, so Vogue Patterns provided a fashion lifeline for owners of sewing machines who wanted to be fashionable, or just wanted to be able to change their wardrobe, at a reasonable cost. Today, shops and stores are everywhere and, with the advent of the internet and on-line shopping, fashion is far more instant and available. In previous years, finding the fashion style you wanted within your budget was much more difficult.

Vogue patterns appeared for the first time in 1905, as an editorial feature in American *Vogue* prompted by a reader's favourite pattern.[40] The mail-order pattern – one size only to begin with – was an instant success; others followed and the Vogue Pattern Company was formed in 1914. Thereafter their popularity grew in tandem with the increasing popularity of *Vogue* itself. In the '30s the *Vogue Pattern Book* came as a separate publication attached to the magazine. During the Second World War, however, all fabrics and materials, including the tissue paper for the patterns, were severely restricted. As part of the war effort there was a special 'Make-do and Mend' section on how to re-vamp old styles as every class of household was forced to eke out and renovate existing clothes. Labour was also in short supply, as production personnel at the company's English manufacturing and distribution arm were diverted from pattern manufacture to more pressing war duties, before a fire bomb during the Blitz destroyed their premises. By the '50s the patterns were included within *Vogue*, along with helpful hints on how to achieve the best dressmaking results. It seems natural that the most influential fashion magazine should reach out in this way to a readership eager to appropriate the latest looks for themselves, whatever their means and wherever they were. *Vogue* pattern buyers were expected to be as fashionably astute as their magazine editor counterparts, constantly in tune with the changing moods and on the look-out for new talent.

The original Vogue Patterns remit was centred around the glamour of stylish dressing. In America, Vogue Patterns had introduced a Hollywood line in 1932 to capitalise on the wide-spread appeal of film star glamour, and this production continued until 1947. However, they wanted to raise the fashion stakes even higher. In Paris that year Christian Dior's 'New Look' mesmerised the fashion press. On the streets of Paris, it caused a near riot – housewives used to wartime strictures revolted against the profligate and extravagant use of fabric in such full-skirted designs by disrupting fashion shoots. In Britain, clothing coupons were still the main fashion currency, but even this couldn't stop the thirst for glamour. In 1949, two years after Dior unveiled his 'New Look', Vogue Patterns announced a significant fashion coup. Creating headline news in the fashion world, they revealed that, for the first time, Paris original models from leading French couturiers would be available as *Vogue* paper patterns. This announcement transformed the paper pattern industry worldwide. Now there would be exact reproductions of original couture styles, allowing women everywhere who could sew or who had access to a good dressmaker to wear Paris fashions at a fraction of the cost. It was a major step forward for the democratisation of fashion and high style. With this move, Vogue Patterns became, and today remains, the only company permitted to purchase couture designs for their international pattern range.

Initially, eight Parisian couturiers were featured, including Jacques Fath, Schiaparelli, and Lanvin, and for a time the emphasis was solely on French designers, just as they dominated fashion in general. Gradually, the rise of new international names and new fashion capitals captured the headlines. In the '60s and '70s Italian, American and British designers like Bellville Sassoon were invited to join the Vogue Patterns galaxy. Over the years many famous names in the fashion

OPPOSITE PAGE Curvaceous glamour for the home dressmaker: body-conscious contours accentuated by a sweeping fishtail hemline [Photograph © The McCall Pattern Company]

world have appeared in the pattern book, among them Dior, Givenchy, Yves Saint Laurent, Valentino, Ungaro, Gianni Versace, Issey Miyake, Geoffrey Beene, Oscar de la Renta, Calvin Klein, Michael Kors and Vera Wang. Today, Bellville Sassoon is the only British company among their international designer roster.

Being a *Vogue* licensee often brought me into contact with their other designers. I remember going to a drinks party given by Jean Muir for the Vogue Patterns team at her new all-white apartment at Albert Court, a redbrick mansion block behind the Royal Albert Hall. I went with John Norman, Russ Norris and Jacqueline Horscher-Thomas from Vogue Patterns. On arrival every guest was asked to remove their shoes as Jean didn't want her beautiful white floor to be marked. It was the '70s and I was wearing very high platform boots and in order to give myself even more height I had put matchboxes in the heels. I did not want to remove my boots and lose my extra inches because my trousers would then be trailing on the floor. So I clomped along the long white hallway leaving black scuff marks on the pristine white floor. Miss Muir was not amused. I felt very uncomfortable and decided to leave. She escorted me to the door and informed me with great displeasure, "You are the only guest who has not removed his shoes!" Needless to say, I was never invited again!

Oscar de la Renta is another designer who has been very successful in the pattern book. I have always admired Oscar; he understands and loves women and this is very apparent in his designs. He makes ultra-feminine, ultra-elegant, flattering clothes that women want to wear. I met him when he came to London to do a charity fashion show at Claridges in the 1980s. Shakira Caine was chairman of the event and asked me to make her a special dress for the occasion. Princess Margaret was guest-of-honour and it was a very glamorous evening. Oscar's wife, Annette looked fabulous in a dress that also appeared on the catwalk, but she managed to look even more beautiful than the model in what was an amazing show.

Our association with Vogue Patterns has developed over the past forty years. Under our contract, each season the expert Vogue Patterns team selects dresses from our latest collection; they know exactly which new designs they are looking for and are very attuned to which styles will appeal to their customers. The company buys copies of the original samples, together with the toile (a mock-up of the finished garment) and the paper pattern, which is then adapted and sized to suit its worldwide distribution. I am always impressed by how quickly Vogue Patterns is able to make these changes, photograph the new styles, and put them in the pattern book.

When designing our collections we make sure that we think of the pattern customer too, and the dresses that will appeal to them are an important consideration. Certain designs can be timeless, and a successful dress can remain in the pattern book for a number of years, thereby becoming a classic. We have always had great success with our evening designs and wedding dresses. These are traditionally complex and expensive purchases, often featuring boned bodices and intricate decorative detailing. The availability of patterns for such specialist styles allow the Vogue Patterns customer to achieve their dream dresses just as our own customers can.

Working with the Vogue Patterns staff has been a very enjoyable experience, and several have become personal friends, in particular, Jacqueline Horscher-Thomas who has for many years run the Paris office. Her twice-yearly buying trips to London were enormous fun and we struck up a great rapport over the forty-odd years we worked together. Her style and French elegance were always perfect. Apart from her natural flair, professionally she had two key talents – a marvellous eye for a good dress and an intuitive feel for the needs of the dressmaking customer.

I always find it very rewarding when I go to a party or reception and see someone wearing one of my designs, especially when it is one that she has made herself from one of our *Vogue* patterns. As Twiggy explains in her autobiography: 'Even now half the pleasure comes from making something for a fraction the price it would cost in the shops. The other pleasure comes from choosing the fabric.'[41] Among the letters we receive, many are from our Vogue Patterns customers, thrilled with their home-made dresses. Their enthusiasm for their projects seems boundless and dedicated, and they often mention how much they enjoy the actual process of dressmaking. 'It's not just clothes. It's sewing itself that I find so creative and satisfying,' agrees Twiggy.[42] One Vogue Patterns enthusiast, however, arrived at our London salon all the way from America and straight from the airport. From her suitcase she produced a part-made dress and asked for advice on how to finish it!

In the 21st century the art of dressmaking still plays a significant role in the fashion world and the sale of high fashion-style paper patterns remains a lucrative global industry. In fact, both 2006 and 2007 have seen a huge surge in the sale of sewing machines; one international company reported a 258% increase during this period. This is due in part to the growing awareness of social and environmental issues, as well as and a move away from the built-in obsolescence of many of today's fashion trends, and women's natural desire to stand out from the crowd.[43] The cult of individuality appeals as much to the home dressmaker as it does to the exclusive world of the couture customer. Women still enjoy the pleasure of having a dress made just for them, whether they have made it themselves or whether someone else has made it for them. Such skills are in real demand and despite the choice available in the shops, a good dressmaker is often the secret behind a well-dressed woman, and worth her weight in gold to her loyal customers. Today, this special craft, with its own cachet and pleasure, thrives all over the world, largely thanks to Vogue Patterns and we are proud to continue to be part of this success.

In October 2008 I will be in Chicago to receive a Lifetime Achievement award from the Association of Sewing and Design Professionals in recognition of our longstanding and highly successful association with Vogue Patterns. As the early years of the new millennium see rising numbers of home dressmakers, the appeal of Bellville Sassoon continues to attract the sartorial imagination of professional and amateur dressmakers all over the world.

OPPOSITE PAGE Stepping out in Bellville Sassoon – home couture style, bustier top with a glitter puffball skirt [Photograph © The McCall Pattern Company]

The season's
best new looks
take charge in
sequins, lace,
tulle and taffeta

286

VOGUE COUTURIER DESIGN

1828
Belinda Bellville
of London

The season's best new looks take charge in sequins, lace, tulle and taffeta

289

Le dúmachas
Larcan ó

MaryMcAleese
Spain 8009

294

BELLVILLE SASSOON
LORCAN MULLANY

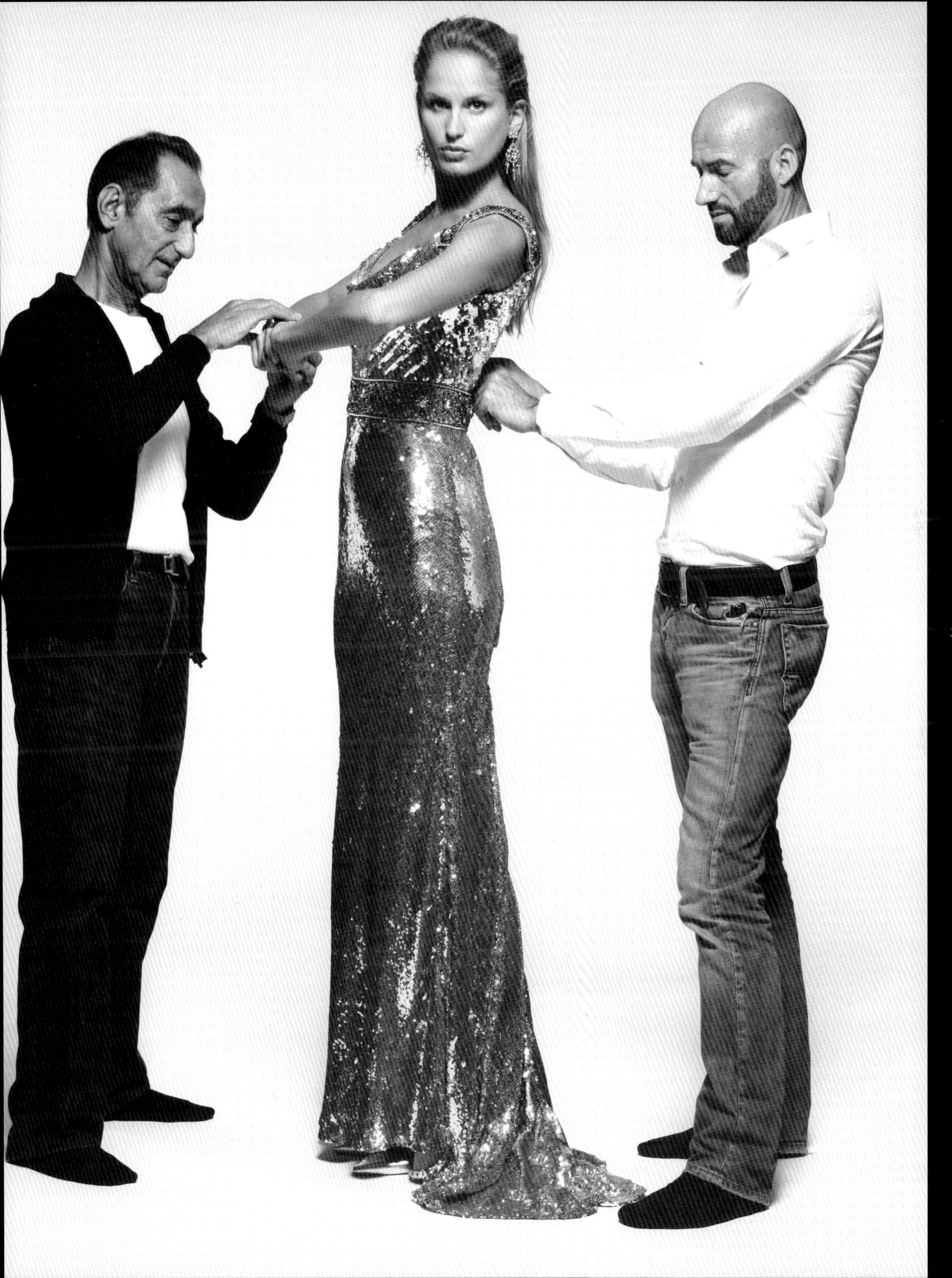

REFERENCES

1
Ernestine Carter, *Sunday Times*,
22 November, 1964

2
Observer, 6 November, 1960

3
Sunday Times, 22 November, 1964

4
Observer, 6 November, 1960

5
Daily Mail, 23 April, 1963

6
Unlabelled magazine cutting,
David Sassoon's archive scrapbook;
Sunday Times, 24 March, 1963

7
Daily Mail, 23 April, 1963

8
The Times, 11 October, 1966

9
Harper's & Queen, September, 1971

10
Feature by Beryl Hartland,
unlabelled cutting from the
Daily Telegraph, 1963,
DS archive scrapbook

11
Women's Wear Daily, 9 July, 1965

12
Women's Wear Daily, 9 July, 1965

13
Sunday Times, 22 November, 1964

14
American *Vogue*, 1963

15
Life magazine, 18 October, 1963

16
Women's Wear Daily, 9 July, 1965

17
British *Vogue*, 14 September, 1970

18
British *Vogue*, November, 1970,
p.115, photographer: Barry Lategan

19
British *Vogue*, May, 1996

20
Unlabelled newspaper cutting,
DS archive scrapbook

21
Unlabelled newspaper cutting,
DS archive scrapbook

22
The Scotsman, 4 May, 1963

23
Daily Express, 17 November, 1966

24
Women's Wear Daily, 22/23, 1965

25
Unlabelled newspaper cutting,
DS archive scrapbook

26
Los Angeles Times, 26 March, 1982

27
Women's Wear Daily, 9 July, 1965

28
Daily Mail, 24 March, 1960

29
Women's Journal, February, 1965

30
Sunday Times, 23 June, 1963

31
Hardy Amies, *Still Here*,
Weidenfeld & Nicholson, 1984

32
British *Vogue*, February 1972;
undated cutting from French *Vogue*,
DS archive scrapbook;
Women's Wear Daily, 2 December, 1971;
Sunday Times, 20 February, 1972

33
British *Vogue*, February 1972

34
Lady Annabel Goldsmith in
private letter to DS, 25 January 2008

35
Sunday Times, 20 February, 1972

36
Evening News, 14 November, 1973

37
Women's Wear Daily, 3 June, 1977

38
British *Vogue*, September 1978

39
Twiggy Lawson with Penelope Denning,
*Twiggy in Black and White – An
Autobiography*, Simon & Shuster Ltd, Great
Britain, 1997,
pp26-27

40
'Behind the Seams at Vogue: The Making
of a Pattern' (The first in a multi-part
series revealing a "Behind-the-Seams"
look
at *Vogue*'s patternmaking process), Vogue
Patterns pattern book, January/February,
1996

41
Twiggy Lawson with Penelope Denning,
*Twiggy in Black and White – An
Autobiography*, Simon & Shuster Ltd, Great
Britain, 1997, p27

42
Twiggy Lawson with Penelope Denning,
*Twiggy in Black and White – An
Autobiography*, Simon & Shuster Ltd, Great
Britain, 1997, p27

43
Daily Telegraph, 28 April, 2008

ACKNOWLEDGEMENTS

We should like to thank everyone who has generously contributed to this book, without whose valuable input it would not have been possible.

We would especially like to acknowledge the specialist design skills of Orna Frommer-Dawson, Geoff Windram, and Cassandra Boehme at John and Orna Designs, who brought their hallmark stylish elegance to this project. Suzy Menkes for her encouragement, and for kindly writing the introduction with her inimitable brio. David Reeson, who generously gave up his time and assisted with picture research. Mark Eastment, Director of V&A Publications, for championing the book in its earliest days. Grateful thanks also go to Diana Steel, Director of ACC Publishing and her team – in particular Susannah Hecht, who acted as editor, for her unstinting support and advice, the ever-sunny-voiced Alison Hart, and the concerted talents and efforts of Tom Conway, Jane Emeny, Juliet Henney, Stephen Mackinlay, Anna Morton, Anna Pearce, Sandra Pond, James Smith, Sarah Smye and Richard Weale.

We would like to thank the many individuals and companies who have kindly given access to their archives and made available images. Rosemary Harden, curator of the Fashion Museum, Bath, and her delightful assistant, Elaine Uttley at the Fashion Museum, Bath, who generously facilitated our research and provided key images; our thanks also go to Bath & North East Somerset Council. Alexandra Shulman and Anna Harvey at British *Vogue* for their enthusiastic support. Harriet Wilson, for her much appreciated kindness and generosity, her efficient and charming assistant, Nicky Budden, and also the wonderfully capable Danielle Yeo at The Condé Nast Publications Ltd, who pulled out all the stops to help us. We are also indebted to the staff of the Condé Nast Library, in particular Brett Croft who is unfailingly courteous and knowledgeable, and also Bonnie Robinson, Jessica Burley, Niki Wood, and Diane Courtney at National Magazine Company, all of whom kindly arranged special access to their archives and provided images. Thanks are also due to Vogue Patterns and The McCall Pattern Company; to Alex Stoke and Sunseekers; Rocio Nogueira at *Hello!* magazine; and Peta Hunt at *You & Your Wedding* magazine.

We are also grateful to Leigh Yule at the Norman Parkinson Archive, June Newton, the Helmut Newton Estate, and Tiggy Maconochie at Maconochie Photography, Diana Donovan and Sarah McIntosh of the Terence Donovan Archive, Joanna Ling and Katherine Marshall of the Cecil Beaton Studio Archive at Sotheby's, Bernard Horrocks at the National Portrait Gallery, Dave McCall at the British Film Institute, Stephen Atkinson at Rex Features, Tim and Eileen Graham, Yianni Vass, Luigi Di Dio, Stacey Smithson, and Martina Oliver at Getty Images, Kezia Storr at PA Photos, and Mark Swift at Express Newspapers.

We would also like to particularly thank the following for their generous contributions: HRH Princess Alexandra, HRH Princess Michael of Kent, President Mary McAleese, Lady Sarah Aspinall, Belinda Bellville, Countess Leopold von Bismarck, Joanne Brogden and Fred Duberry, Mrs Charmian Campbell, Marquess of Cholmondeley, Lady Annabel Goldsmith, Virginia Ironside, Mrs Jane Stevens, Blaine Trump, Mrs Dawn Wells.

Very special thanks go to Barry Lategan, Roxanne Lowit, Patrick MacMullan, and Terry O'Neill.

ILLUSTRATIONS

Anneliese
p. 256, 257 (*Women's Wear Daily*
© Condé Nast Publications)
Sheena Carslaw
pp. 42, 43, 64, 68, 69, 74, 78, 82, 84–85,
101, 170, 176, 248
(top row 3 illustrations), 249
(top row far left), 258, 259, 264
Richard Cawley:
pp. 192, 193, 206, 208, 210–211
Romy Gelardin
pp. 142–143, 144, 160, 248 (bottom row
3 illustrations), 249 (bottom row 3
illustrations), 268–269, 272, 296
Beryl Hartland
p. 69 (*Daily Telegraph*, 8 July 1964)
Francis Marshall
p. 158 (undated cutting from *Daily
Mail*, David Sassoon Archive
scrapbook)
George Sharp
pp. 129, 134, 135, 137, 139, 164, 183, 184,
185, 190, 196, 200, 215, 216, 218, 220,
222
Stephen Stipelman
p. 228 (*Women's Wear Daily* © Condé
Nast Publications)
Helen Storey
pp. 112, 114, 115 (background wall
of sketches), 120–121, 124–125, 128,
165, 186, 194, 202, 212, 213, 214

PHOTOGRAPHIC CREDITS

Clive Arrowsmith
Chris Ashford
David Bailey
Cecil Beaton
Robyn Beeche
Jonathan Buckmaster
Hugo Burnand
John Carter
Alex Chatelain
Willie Christie
Ben Coster
John Cowan
Reginald Davis, MBE
Terence Donovan
John Dormer
Fred Duberry
Arthur Elgort
Robert Erdmann
John French
William Garrett
Tim Graham
Danilo Giuliani
Jenny Hands
Kayt Jones
Dmitri Kasterine
Mark Kauffman
Brien Kirley
Natalie de Lamoral
Barry Lategan
Trevor Leighton
Patrick Lichfield
Roxanne Lowit
Stefano Massimo
Tony McGee
Patrick MacMullan
Michel Molinare
David Montgomery
Rebecca Naden
Helmut Newton
Desmond O'Neill
Terry O'Neill
David Olins
Alberto dell 'Orto
Norman Parkinson
Christa Peters
Iain Philpott
Mike Reinhardt
Angus Ross
Eva Sereny
Mark Stewart
John Swannell
Toscani
Charlie Troman
Bruce Weber
James Wedge
Susan Wood
John Young

INDEX
*Page numbers in ital refer to
illustrations and/or captions*

Aberdare, Lady 264

Academy Awards *see*: Oscars

Alexander I, Tsar of Russia 252

Alexandra, Princess *163-167*; 47, 70, 156-157, 162, 168, 180, 192, 264, 266

Alice of Gloucester, Princess *see*: Gloucester

Amies, Hardy 26, 34, 114, 156, 174, 252

Andrews, Julie 114

Anne, Princess *158-161*; *158-159*, 162, 184, 264

Anne-Marie, ex-Queen of Greece 88

Arbeid, Murray 88

Armani Privé 269

Armstrong Jones, Anthony *see*: Snowdon, Earl of

Armstrong Jones, Lady Sarah 213

Arrowsmith, Clive 64

Ashley, Laura 100

Ashton, Lady *see*: Garland, Madge

Aspinall, Lady Sarah *see*: Courage, Lady Sarah

Astor, Lady *see*: Pugh, Bronwen

Attenborough, Sir Richard 157

Bacall, Lauren 47

Baghdad 10, 14

Bailey, David *74*, *84*, 130, *171*; 64, 68

Balenciaga, Cristobal 26, 28, 31, 106

Balmain, Pierre 31, 41

Baryshnikov, Mikhail 271

Bashi family 47

Bassey, Dame Shirley *134*

Bates, John 46, 88

Bazaar (*see also*: Mary Quant) 28, 34, 64

Beatles, The 179

Beaton, Cecil *23*, *54*, *70-71*; 23, 159, 180, 260, 263

Beatrix, Queen of The Netherlands 201

Beatty, Lady *37*, *38*, *262*, *263*; 41, 263, 264

Beckwith-Smith, Anne 192

Beene, Geoffrey 192, 283

belle époque see: Proust theme

Bellville, Belinda, *35*, *38*, *39*, *50*, *51*, *53*, *57*, *60-61*, *234*, *244*; 31-54, 68-70, 88, 106, 140, 156, 158, 168, 174, 180, 186, 188, 192, 215, 228, 252, 253, 260, 264, 265, 266, 278

Bellville, Camilla 228

Bellville et Cie *48*, *49*, *158*, *248*, *254*, *255*; 34, 40

Berenson, Marisa 64, 68, 263

Bergdorf Goodman 47, 228

Bergen, Candice *84-85*; 47, 64

Berkeley Debutantes Dress Show *50*; 46

Betjeman, Candida *237*, *228*; 228

Biba (*see also*: Hulanicki, Barbara) 46, 64, 70, 265

Birley, Lady Annabel (Lady Annabel Goldsmith) 263

Blass, Bill 130

Boughton, David *140*; 140

Boyd, John 192

Brogden, Joanne *23*; 16, 18, 31

Brook, Kelly 273

Bruce, Evangeline (Mrs David Bruce) *54*; 46, 157

Burton, Sir Richard *171*; 100

Bussell, Darcey 119

Butler and Wilson 188, 260

Caine, Michael 266

Caine, Shakira *252*; 106, 266, 283

Calvin Klein 130, 283

Campbell-Walter, Fiona *see*: von Thyssen, Baroness

Cannes Film Festival *273*; 269

Capote, Truman 102

Capri 23

Capucci, Roberto 26

Cardin, Pierre 28, 31, 68

Carnaby Street 46, 64, 70

Carter, Ernestine 40, 54, 70, 228

Cartier 41, 253

Cartland, Barbara 106

Casati, Marchesa 263

Cavanagh, John 23, 26

Cawley, Richard *92*, *102*; 88, 114

Chambers, Lucinda *140*

Chambre Syndicale de la Couture, Paris 26, 28

Chanel, Gabrielle 'Coco' 28, 31, 41, 214, 269

Chanel, House of 28, 31, 41, 214, 269

Charles, Prince (Prince of Wales) *156*, *187*, *188*, *191*, *201*; 158, 168, 188, 193, 214

Chelsea, Viscount *235*, *236*

Chelsea Embankment 64

Christie, Julie *76*; 64

Christie's, New York *218*, *220*; 213, 215

Clark, Ossie 28, 46, 114

Coke, Viscountess *see*: Whately, Polly

Colin, Pamela *see*: Harlech, Lady

Collins, Joan 214

Cornwall, Duchess of *see*: Shand, Camilla

Courage, Lady Sarah (Aspinall, Lady Sarah; Curzon, Lady Sarah) *231*; 263

Courrèges, André 28, 68, 263

Courtaulds 23

Crawford, Cindy *117*

Curzon, Lady Sarah *see*: Courage, Lady Sarah

Daily Mail *216*; 228

Dali, Salvador 263

de la Renta, Annette 283

de la Renta, Oscar 283

Deneuve, Catherine (Mrs David Bailey) *77*

Deniz, Liese *229*, *254*, *255*

Derby, Lady *38*

Dessès, Jean 26, 28, 31, 68

Devonshire, Duchess of 266

Diana, Princess of Wales *156*, *157*, *186-255*; 106, 114, 130, 156, 157, 162, 168, 174, 184, 186-215, 230

Dickinson, Janice *105*

Dior, Christian 23, 26, 28, 31, 34, 41, 46, 174, 214, 263, 269, 282, 283

Donovan, Terence 64

du Bois, Nena *39*

du Pré, Jacqueline 106

Duberry, Fred *23*

Dunaway, Faye 64, 106

Ebury, Lady *38*

Eden, Anthony 34

Egypt 16

Ekland, Britt 68

Elizabeth II, Queen *24-25*, *166*, *187*; 22, 156-157, 158-159, 174, 184, 186, 188, 192, 193, 215, 264, 265

Epstein, Brian 179

Evangelista, Linda 130

Ewart, Keith 40

Fath, Jacques 282

Fattal family 140

Felipe, Crown Prince of Spain 292

Festival of Britain (1951) 22

Finney, Albert *42*

Fleming, Anne 260

Foale, Marion 47; 28, 46

Fontana Sisters, The 26

Forsberg, Joan 162

Fortnum & Mason 47

Fox, Freddie 88

Frankel, Anna 22

Fraser, Honor 130

Fratini, Gina 88

Friel, Anna 140

Galitzine, Princess Irene 26

Garavino, Valentino *see*: Valentino

Gardner, Ava 100

Garland, Madge (Lady Ashton) *23*; 18, 23, 26, 28

Gaultier, Jean Paul 269

Gelardin, Romy *140*; 140

Gibb, Bill 28, 88, 114

Ginger Group 64

Givenchy, Hubert de 28, 263, 283

Glass-Hooper, Sevilla *see*: Hercolani, Princess Sevilla 55

Glenconner, Lady (Lady Anne Tennant) *257*; 264

Gloucester, Duchess of 157, 264

Gloucester, Princess Alice of 157

Gloucester Cathedral, *203*; 212

Goff, Trish 130

Golden Globe Awards, 269

Goldsmith, Lady Annabel *see*: Birley, Lady Annabel

Granny Takes a Trip 70

Grès, Madame 28

Grosvenor, Lady Leonora 264

Guirey, Princess 264

Gunning, Anne *44-45*; 41

Halston 102

Hammersmith School of Art *18*, *19*; 16-18, 22, 28, 31, 47

Hammond, Celia 64

Harlech, Lady (Pamela Colin) 46, 266

Harlow, Shalom 130

Harmsworth, Sarah *228*; 228

Harper's Bazaar *66*, *67*, *236*; 16, 46, 100, 130

Harpers and Queen *90*, *97*, *122*, *126*, *127*, *133*, *138*, *145*; 46

Harrods *205*; 47, 263

Hartland, Beryl 69

Hartnell, Norman 106, 156, 174

Heim, Jacques 68

Hepburn, Audrey *42*; 47, 68

Hercolani, Princess Sevilla (Sevilla Glass-Hooper) 41

Herrera, Carolina 130

Hicks, David *158*; 158, 252

Hicks, Lady Pamela (Lady Pamela Mountbatten) *158*, *257*; 158, 252, 264

Horrocks 22

Horscher-Thomas, Jacqueline *288*; 283, 284

Howard, Lady Mary Fitzalan 264

Hulanicki, Barbara (*see also*: Biba) 64, 265

Humphries, Avril 26

Incorporated Society of London Fashion Designers 23, 44, 174

Ironside, Janey *23*, *30*; 28

Jackson, Betty 278

Jagger, Bianca 102, 106

Jeff, Walter *102*; 102

Jenkins, Katherine 140

Jennifer's Diary (*see also*: Betty Kenward) 54, 228

John, Elton 266

Johnson, President Lyndon B. 177

Juan Carlos, King of Spain 293

Karan, Donna 130

Kasterine, Dmitri *53*, *54*

Kelly, Grace *see*: Monaco, Princess Grace of

Kennedy, Jacqueline 46

Kennington, Jill 64; 64

Kent, Duchess of (Katherine Worsley) *168-173*; 47, 88, 157, 158, 168-173, 188, 192

Kent, Duke of *171*; 158

Kent, Prince Michael of *181*, *182*; 180

Kent, Princess Michael of (Baroness Marie-Christine von Reibnitz) *180-183*; 157, 180-183

Kenward, Betty (*see also*: *Jennifer's Diary*) 54

Kenzo Takada 70

Khan, Begum Aga 47

Klein, Bernat 175

Klein, Calvin 130, 283

Klein, Roland 88

Kors, Michael 283

Lacroix, Christian 114, 269

Lagerfeld, Karl 102

Lambton, Lady *94*; 88, 100

Lancetti, House of 114

Lanvin, House of 68, 263, 282

Lategan, Barry *93*, *94*, *104*, *242*; 64

Laura Ashley *see*: Ashley, Laura

Laurencin, Marie 23

Le Bon, Yasmin *108*

Leith, Mrs Gordon 'Cuckoo' 34, 265

Lewis, Leona 140

Life magazine *47*, *177*; 64

Loewenstein, Princess *263*; 263

Londonderry, Lady *60-61*, *96*; 252

Londonderry, Lord 253

Londonderry, Marchioness of 252

Londonderry House 41

Londonderry jewels 252-253

Lord Chamberlain 34

Louis Vuitton 14

Louis XVI, King of France 252

Lycett Green, Rupert 237

Macdonald, Julien 130

Macmillan, Harold 34

Madonna, *135*

Madge Garland (Lady Ashton) *23*; 18, 23, 26, 28

Margaret, Princess *59*, *175-179*, *201*, *261*; 47, 156, 157, 174-179, 252, 265, 283

Margarethe, Queen of Sweden 88

302

Marie Antoinette
Queen of France 252

Marie Chantal of Greece, Princess 274

Marina, Princess 162, 180

Marks & Spencer 23

Martineau, Lindy 228; 228

Mattli, House of 26

McAleese, Mary 293; 292

McAlpine, Mrs William 266

McCann, Gerald 46, 88, 265

McDowell, Andie, 238-239

McFadden, Mary 130

McQueen, Alexander 130

Michael 26

Michael, Princess
see: Kent, Princess Michael of

Miller, Beatrix, 68, 180

Miller, Melanie 68

Minnelli, Liza 102

Mirman, Simone 23

Miyake, Issey 102, 283

Mizrahi, Isaac 130

Molinare, Michel 44, 45, 48, 49, 254, 255

Molyneux, House of 23

Monaco, Princess Grace of
(Grace Kelly) 263, 266

Monroe, Marilyn 22

Montagu Douglas Scott, Charmian
(Charmian Stirling) 58, 231

Montgomery, David 57, 67, 75, 79; 64

Morton, Digby 22, 26

Moss, Martin
(see also: Woollands) 47

Mountbatten, Lord and Lady 158, 252

Mountbatten, Lady Pamela
see: Lady Pamela Hicks

Mr Freedom 70

Muir, Jean 47, 46, 64, 88, 265, 278, 283

Mullany, Lorcan 107, 292; 114, 130, 140

National Service 16

Nevill, Angela 265

Nevill, Bernard, 100, 101

Nevill, Lady Rupert 38

Noor, Queen of Jordan 88, 260

Norman, John 283

Norris, Russ 283

Nureyev, Rudolf 195

O'Neill, Terry 132; 106

O'Reilly, Pat 36

Oberon, Merle 13; 10, 14

Olivier, Laurence 10

Onassis, Jackie 266

Oppenheim, Lady 38

Ormsby-Gore, Lady 264

Ortiz Rocasolano, Letizia 292

Osbourne, Kelly 140

Osbourne, Sharon 140

Oscars, 266

Parkinson, Norman 47, 89, 182, 235, 240, 241, 261; 64, 180

Paterson, Ronald 26

Philip, Prince 184, 264

Phillips, Lucienne 14

Picture Post 16

Pike, Rosamund 140

Pleydell-Bouverie, Hon. Mrs Peter 40

Plunket Greene, Alexander 265

Proust theme (belle époque) 98, 99, 262-264; 14, 260-263

Pugh, Bronwen
(Lady Astor) 48, 49; 41

Quant, Mary 47; 28, 34, 44, 46, 64, 265

Queen magazine 29, 57, 59, 65, 73, 235, 253, 261

RADA
(Royal Academy of Dramatic Art) 14

Radziwill, Princess Lee 46

Rayne, Lady Jayne 264

Redgrave, Vanessa 47, 168

Rhodes, Zandra 130, 152, 252; 54, 88, 114, 130, 180

Ritblat, Jill 43

Roberts, Michael 188

Rogers, Shannon 265

Rollerina 102

Rothermere, Lady 'Bubbles' 106

Rothermere, Lord 106

Rothschild, Baron Guy de 263; 260-263

Rothschild, Baronne Marie-Hélène 263; 260-263

Royal Air Force 17; 16

Royal College of Art (see also: School
of Fashion Design) 22, 24-25, 26, 27, 29,
30; 16, 18, 22-23, 28, 31, 41, 44, 263

Royal School of Needlework, 238

Royal Variety Show 168

Rudolf 23

Saatchi family 47

Saint Laurent, Yves 31, 34, 41, 64, 68,
70, 102, 174, 263, 283

Saks Fifth Avenue 130; 102, 130

Sargent, John Singer 13; 14, 18, 260

Sassoon family:
David, 16, 17, 19, 29, 30, 35, 47, 50, 52,
57, 60-61, 88, 102, 106, 107, 130, 132,
134, 140, 152-153, 159, 180, 224-225,
230, 288, 292, 297; passim
Gourgi (David's father) 11; 10, 14, 16, 18
Laurette (David's sister) 10
Marguerite
(Lady Woolf; David's sister) 12, 16,
270; 10, 14, 16, 23, 106
Mollie (David's sister) 17; 10, 16
Ronald (David's brother) 10, 106
Victor (David's brother) 10
Victoria (David's mother) 11; 10

Sassoon, Flora 10

Sassoon, Lady Aline 13; 14, 18

Sassoon, Vidal 265

Saxones 22

Schiaparelli, Elsa 28, 263, 282

School of Fashion Design
Royal College of Art (Fashion School)
16, 22, 23, 28, 31

Scott, Mrs Sydna 'Scottie' 40, 41, 158

Sekers, Miki 23

Sellers, Miranda 68

Sellers, Peter 68

Serpentine Gallery 114

Seymour, Stephanie 130

Shand, Camilla
(Duchess of Cornwall) 41

Shand Kydd, Frances 186, 188, 192

Sharp, George 131, 230; 114

Shenkman, Belle 106

Shrimpton, Jean 70-71; 64, 68

Sibley, Dame Antoinette 47

Silverman, Jerry 265

Sim, Sheila 157

Sinatra, Frank 100

Sitwell family, 23

Snowdon, Earl of
(Anthony Armstrong Jones) 174, 180

Soraya, ex-Queen of Iran 88

Springfield, Dusty 47, 68, 134

Stephens, John 46, 64

Stevens, Jane 59, 261; 180, 264, 265

Stevens, Jocelyn 59, 257, 261

Stirling, Archie 230

Stirling, Charmian
see: Montagu Douglas Scott, Charmian

Storey, David 114

Storey, Helen 114; 114

Streisand, Barbra 134

Studio 54 102

Styler, Trudi 130

Suez Crisis 16

Sunday Times 232, 236-237; 40, 54, 70, 228, 260, 263

Swann, Moyra 84

Tatler 50, 188

Tavistock, Marchioness of
(Henrietta Tiarks) 34

Taylor, Elizabeth 100-101, 171, 207; 47, 100, 106, 174, 263

Te Kanawa, Kiri 134

Tennant, Lady Anne
see: Glenconner, Lady

Tennant, Stella 130

Testino, Mario 272

Thaarup, Aage 23

Thatcher, Margaret 106

Thomas, Merrill 252; 106

Tiarks, Henrietta
see: Tavistock, Marchioness of

Tidmarsh, Christine 41

Tilberis, Liz 130; 130

Times, The 46

Tosi, Piero 263

Treacy, Philip 130

Tree, Penelope 84; 64, 68

Trump, Blaine 271, 274, 275; 266

Tuffin, Sally 47; 28, 46

TV-AM 106

Twiggy 64, 278, 284

UK Fashion Export Council 159

Ungaro, Emanuel 283

Valentino (Valentino Garavani) 114, 140, 263, 283

Venice Film Festival 269

Versace, Gianni 214, 283

Versen, Miss Alexandra 255; 269

Villeneuve, Justin de 64

Visconti, Luchino 263

Vogue, American 55; 64, 282, 283

Vogue, British 70-71, 75, 77, 79, 80, 81,
83, 84, 85, 86, 87, 89, 91, 92, 94, 95, 98,
99, 104, 105, 116, 117, 118, 140, 171, 182,
272; 14, 16, 23, 46, 47, 50, 68, 70, 100,
130, 180, 260, 263, 266

Vogue, French 260

Vogue Brides 240, 241, 242-243

Vogue Patterns 278, 280-281, 286-289;
68, 278-284

von Bismarck, Countess 230

von Bülow, Claus 41

von Pallandt, Felicia 245

von Reibnitz, Baroness Marie-Christine
see: Kent, Princess Michael of

von Thyssen, Baroness
(Fiona Campbell-Walter) 41

Vreeland, Diana 64, 130

Vuitton see: Louis Vuitton

Wales, Prince of
see: Charles, Prince

Wales, Princess of
see: Diana, Princess of Wales

Wallop, Lady Philippa 228, 235, 236;
228, 264

Wang, Vera 283

Warhol, Andy 102

Wells, Dawn 234

West Cumberland Silk Mills 23

Westminster, Duchess of 38

Wha Chung, Kyung 134; 134

Whately, David 40

Whately, Polly
(Viscountess Coke) 244

Whittle, Andrew 94, 95; 88

Windsor, Duchess of 23, 263

Windsor, Duke of 23

Windsor, Lady Helen 168, 192

Windsor Castle 161, 210, 261; 157, 159, 264

Woman's Journal 228

Women's Wear Daily 34, 39, 103, 228,
229, 256, 257, 262; 47, 50, 54, 68, 174,
228, 260, 264

Woolf, Lady
see: Sassoon family, Marguerite

Woollands
(see also: Moss, Martin) 47, 228

Worsley, Katherine
see: Kent, Duchess of

Yentob family 47

York, Duchess of 184-185; 157, 184

York, Duke of 184; 184

Young, Richard 188

Ziff, Robina 214

Zilkha family 47

303